CROSSING THE HIDDEN BRIDGE

CHRISTIANS OF THE HOLYLAND

TONY MUBARAK

THE PAPER HOUSE
PUBLISHING

Crossing the Hidden Bridge: Christians of the Holyland
Copyright © 2023 by Tony Mubarak

Published by Twins Tours & Travel Ltd.

All rights reserved. No part of this publication may be reproduced, stored in a retrieval system, or transmitted in any form of by any means- electronic, mechanical, photocopy, recording, or any other- except for brief quotations in printed reviews, without the proper permission of the authors.

Paperback ISBN: 978-1-7348402-4-7
Hardcover ISBN: 978-1-7348402-5-4
eBook ISBN: 978-1-7348402-6-1

All Scripture quotations, unless otherwise indicated, are taken from the New King James Version®. Copyright © 1982 by Thomas Nelson. Used by permission. All rights reserved.

Internet addresses (Websites, YouTube channels, etc.) are offered as resources. The publisher does not guarantee their continued viability over the life of this book.

Interior Design: The Paper House
Cover Design: The Paper House

First printing in 2023

Contents

Acknowledgments vii
My Family ix
Introduction: xi

Part One
Discovering the Hidden Bridge

1. Jesus—The Foundation 3
2. Sources of the Divide—Historical Background 25

Part Two
The Hidden Bridge and its Parts

3. Who are the Holyland Christians? 59
4. Christians in Israel Proper 71
5. Christians of the West Bank and Gaza Strip 89
6. Christians from Jerusalem 121
7. Christian Believers from a Muslim Background 153
8. Christian Believers from a Jewish Background 179

Part Three
The Hidden Bridge Revealed

9. The Christian Arab Theology 209
10. The Parable of the Good Samaritan 235

Epilogue 249

Bibliography 261
Additional Information and Resources 263

For Andre, my twin brother. I am incredibly grateful for my brother. Without him, this book would not have been a reality.

He was always ready to help with anything I needed.

Acknowledgments

Writing a book is a community effort, and I am grateful for each person who has helped along the way. I would first like to thank Twins Tours & Travel LTD. for its professional, personal, and financial support.

Likewise, I am deeply indebted to the mentors and teachers who have shaped my understanding of the topics in this book. I look back to my days at Bethlehem Bible College and at my Tour Guide course with the Archeological Seminars Institute in Jerusalem with gratitude.

While my professors are too many to name individually, be assured that you helped lay the foundation of my understanding of the bible. I am grateful. Special thanks go to Dr. Jim Fleming. He will recognize many biblical insights he shared with me years ago in my qualification courses to become a licensed tour guide. Mrs. Maayan Raveh helped me understand Palestinian Christian Theology in a practical way. Her insights are woven throughout Chapter 9.

I owe a special thanks to Kenny Schmitt for reading several drafts of the book. He offered many valuable suggestions and insights. He gave the book organization and structure. I also thank Affordable Christian Editing for helping fix my grammar mistakes. Each of these individuals has contributed to the quality and value of this book.

I want to give special thanks to all of my church community and friends who have kept me in their prayers and given me encouragement throughout this journey. Last—and most importantly—I would like to thank my family. My wife, Sawsan, has been patient and supportive. She has given so much time to help write this book. Of course, I can't forget my son Joseph who at the time of this writing is 17 years old and my daughter Kareen who is already 15 years old.

Each of you kept me going. Thank you!

My Family

My Joseph, me Tony, Sawsan my wife and Kareen my daughter

Introduction:
Crossing the Hidden Bridge

Grandpa's Strolls

As a child, I often heard stories of how my grandfather loved nothing more than going on a *"sarha"*, the Aramaic word for a stroll. He loved striking out in nature on his strolls with family, traversing his vast land and the mountains as he pointed out the ancient paths. The family would take a few provisions for the day and walk through the open hills with no specific destination, leaving behind the burdens of life.

Growing up in Jerusalem, I always had this inner feeling and desire to explore new places. I'm sure it came from my grandfather's love for his strolls. I found refuge in escaping the craziness of the city and taking a break, especially during the holidays. I still have that desire today. I often travel to the north with my wife Sawsan, or Shoshana, (which means in Hebrew the Iris flower) and our two kids, Joseph and Kareen. We typically find ourselves in Haifa, Sawsan's hometown. And even in the north, I find myself longing for a stroll, for escape.

Introduction:

I usually go out to the vast area of Mount Carmel near Haifa. In the mountains, I wonder aimlessly, unrestricted by time or space, moving freely without restraint, following where my spirit takes me. As someone who enjoys thinking and being alone, walking always helps me put things into perspective. These strolls nourish my soul—they help me let go.

When I started strolling alone, I often lost my way. As a kid, grandpa's comments about the ancient paths had never been as interesting as throwing rocks or playing. I took numerous before I found an eye for the ancient paths. But once found them, I regularly encountered prehistoric caves and ancient rock formations.

Each time I ventured further and further into the hills, discovering my thoughts, finding new terrain. The wildflowers always caught my eye, too, showing themselves to me in new ways. Every walk was an adventure—the ancient paths and the beauty of nature, were my personal invitations to meditation.

One time, with the Mediterranean Sea as the backdrop and scattered clouds making a blue-sky pop, I scrambled along some rocks until I lost the ancient path. But I wasn't concerned. The quiet stroll was making me better. The farther I went, the deeper I felt the silence. I found myself sitting on a rain-smoothed rock perched on an overlook. I sat soaking in the view of the sea, the valley, the sky, and the mountains that lay before me.

I was on Mount Carmel that day. The name Carmel comes from two Hebrew words, "*Kerem*" and "*El*". Together, they mean 'Vineyard of God.' The scene before me was proof that the person who named this place did so aptly.

As I soaked in the scene and my eyes scanned the horizon, I noticed a small opening. And hidden there between the trees, a small bridge

Introduction:

came into focus. The narrow structure hung between two terraces in the distance, with no supports in the middle, connecting the footpath between the terraces.

Silent and steadfast, the bridge looked solid and safe to walk on, built to make people's passage between the hills easier. A gentle breeze blew on my face, and my body relaxed. I felt a sense of peace come upon me, perfect. *Then a thought struck me—**Could this bridge be me?***

I decided I needed a closer look. So slowly and carefully, keeping close to the earth, I began making my way to the bridge. As I scrambled between rocks and trees, bushes and flowers, my feet found their way back to the ancient path. Although it was overgrown, I had rediscovered the ancient way. From that point on, the ancient trail showed me the way, and I walked with calm confidence toward my destination. The bridge slowly moved from the horizon to the foreground of my vision.

As I approached it, I realized the bridge was not small as it had seemed from a distance. It was massive. The bridge seemed steady and capable of bearing my weight as I stood in front of it. Yet I hesitated. Should I step onto it? My heart began to race. Was I brave enough to cross? It took a few minutes, but my heart eventually returned to a normal rate, and I took a step of faith.

The wooden planks protested my footfalls with squeaks, but they remained stable. Once I reached the center, I paused again. The view was spectacular. Beyond the valley and slopes below, I could now see vistas of the city of Haifa nested between the green pine mountains. How had I not discovered this hidden bridge before? So close to the city, yet calm and impressive. Hard to find but breathtaking.

You may be thinking that you'd like to stand on this bridge, too. The good news is that the walk to it is pretty easy, and most people could

INTRODUCTION:

reach it without a problem. It's close to the city, though is hidden in the mountain but the trail is steady. And even though, to some, the thought of crossing a bridge hidden in the wilderness might seem intimidating or terrifying, I can assure you it is sturdy and safe. I have now walked it several times, and the view is totally worth it.

The bad news is that there are almost no signs pointing the way to this bridge. The path leading would be almost impossible to find on your own. Even if someone showed you the trailhead and got you started, you would likely get lost since you have not spent a lifetime strolling through the Carmel mountains or been taught how to discover the ancient paths by your grandfather. The path may be easy to walk, but it's often hard to see. If you really wanted to find it, I would suggest you take a guide.

I'm Tony. I'll Be Your Guide

Before I introduce myself in the proper Middle Eastern way, I want to return to the question that struck me sitting on the rain-smoothed rock the day I found the hidden bridge—Could this bridge be me?

That day, even as I strolled the ancient paths and discovered the bridge, I could think of nothing more exciting than sharing the journey and experience with others. That bridge helped me see the beauty of God's vineyard in a new way—from a new perspective. I felt the need to show others. I decided to dedicate my life to helping others find the hidden bridge that day.

But it was more than that. I felt God was telling me something about my life purpose and calling. Could I be part of this hidden bridge that links different people and helps bring peace?

In the Holyland, it's easy to discuss politics and division. War is in the news daily. Arabs and Jews are locked in a zero-sum battle for the land.

Introduction:

They are separated by a deep valley, a great chasm that prevents them from making peace. That day, I felt like God had put something on my life, that I was called to be part of that hidden bridge, an agent of peace.

The more I thought about it, the more I realized that that calling was not only directed at me personally. It was for all of the Christians of the Holyland. The calling to be the hidden bridge was for anyone who followed the teachings of Jesus and believed in his crucifixion, death, and resurrection. In other words, the people who follow Jesus in the Holyland are the hidden bridge. We have discovered the ancient path of his teachings and have found new life as we walk toward him.

Building a bridge is a communal affair, and Jesus is the foundation. And all his followers have kept their faith and heritage. They have journeyed together with Christ through the generations, building upon the foundation of his life and teachings, death and resurrection. They have worked tirelessly through the ages, shaping the bridge according to the divine master's plan.

With this book, I would like to help you to discover the way of Christ as lived out by the Christians of the Holyland. In a place where it is tempting to make judgments about who is right and who is wrong in the Israel-Palestine conflict, I would like to invite you to understand both sides through the eyes of local Christians. Only by doing this we can know the truth. Then the truth will set us free. Only then we can solve the problem.

Reading this book will take you on the ancient path toward the hidden bridge. I'll be your guide. But once we get to the bridge, you'll have to take your own steps onto it. You will need to face the challenge and the decision to continue to cross over it, to experience the beauty of the view for yourself. Having been there, I can assure you that the journey and view are totally worth it.

INTRODUCTION:

Now, let me introduce myself properly—in the true Middle Eastern way.

I am from the Mubarak family of Jerusalem. This is how Jesus was introduced: Jesus of Nazareth, Nathanael of Cana, Mary of Magdalah, and Joseph of Arimathea. In the East, your family name and where you come from are what really matter. Your family name serves as your reputation, especially in small communities. I grew up in the Old City of Jerusalem, where everybody knew each other, and the reputation of each family was what mattered. This is how things work here in the Middle East.

The Mubaraks are a very small Christian family in Jerusalem. With my extended family still living in Jerusalem, we barely come to twenty people. Why are we so few, and how are our numbers getting smaller? We are tiny compared to the other religions, of Orthodox Jews, and of large Muslim communities, whose extended families include at least one hundred and up to six hundred members, counting the men only.

My family name, Mubarak, is Arabic, but it comes originally from Aramaic, meaning blessings, and also from the Hebrew word *"Brakhim"* built off the same root, which literally means knees. Thus, my name, the Blessed (Mubarak), indicates that my blessings come only by kneeling and praying. I am devout and quiet, dedicated to my family and work. I'm secure in my relationship with God and my church.

Tony is my given first name, and I am a Christian Arab. Notice I am a Christian first and then an Arab. Arab is an ethnicity and not a religion. My faith is more important to me than my nationality. My family and I come from a Maronite Catholic background. The Maronite Church is an Eastern Catholic order that is part of Syriac Christianity by heritage. But I consider myself a maronite with a small 'm' since I only attend my traditional Maronite Church (located on a

INTRODUCTION:

small street inside the Jaffa Gate) on high holidays, such as Christmas and New Year's Day.

At the same time, I attend the Alliance Missionary Evangelical Church in the Old City of Jerusalem weekly. The Alliance Missionary Church is located in the heart of the Christian Quarter of the Old City of Jerusalem where I grew up. The church was started in Jerusalem in 1890 by two American Missionaries and has spread to almost eighty more countries worldwide.

Yes, Christians exist in the Middle East. I was never a Muslim or a Jew, so I never converted to Christianity. I was born in Jerusalem and raised as a Christian. In fact, there have always been Christian communities in the Middle East since the times of Jesus. Israel or Palestine, Lebanon, Syria, Jordan, Egypt, and Iraq are all home to various communities of Aramean Christians who were here even before Islam came into existence.

Also, in this land, when a baby is born in a hospital, even before asking the name, the doctors ask the parents' religion. Everyone's nationality is determined by their religion. This illustrates how important religion is in this part of the world. This is how we look at each other in this land, by putting people in religious categories. So yes, Tony is my real name. It was never Moshe or Muhammad. My aunt is Helen, my uncle is John, and my grandmother's name is Mary. I am a Christian Arab.

Professionally, I am a licensed tour guide. Being in this profession for over twenty years, I have collected a wealth of knowledge and experiences. Through my studies, reading, teaching, touring, and meeting people from all over the world—not to mention my background as an Arab Christian from Jerusalem—I have gained a unique perspective on Christianity and the Bible. Thus, in this book, I want to share with you some of the knowledge, experience, and

INTRODUCTION:

insights that have shaped my life and helped change the lives of thousands of tourists that I have guided.

It might not surprise you that one impetus for me to write this book was the COVID-19 pandemic. As the world quaked in 2020 and 2021, I felt I had no time to waste. But this was ironic since the tourist industry had come to a screeching halt, and all I had was time.

It was the first time in so many years that I wasn't too busy. And I felt I needed to use my time wisely. So, I wrote this book. I wanted to write about Christians of the Holyland and let the world know about our small community so people could understand our role and importance in the Kingdom of God.

Not only that, but the pandemic also showed me how connected and dependent everyone in the whole world is. Humanity can't continue to live in small, segregated boxes anymore. Every human is related and dependent upon their neighbor for survival. We must help one another. This book was my way to help.

The pandemic also opened my eyes to the importance of the Christian church in a fresh way. We Christians have a job to stand with our Muslim and Jewish neighbors, allowing God's mercy to be revealed to them. The virus attacked indiscriminately, caring not for race, creed, gender, or social status. The simple citizen was no different from the prime minister. We were all vulnerable. I came to see that all Christians can and should be part of the hidden bridge. We must pray for God's mercy upon every person, whether Jewish, Christian, Muslim, or any other religious tradition.

INTRODUCTION:

THE JOURNEY BEFORE US

What is ahead of us on this journey? Before I answer this question, I would like to make three brief comments.

First, I am aware that most people who come to the Holyland are not geographers, historians, or theologians. For Pilgrims and visitors, come from many professional backgrounds and have vastly different experiences and levels of knowledge about the Bible, Christianity, and the Middle East.

I have written this book to be read and enjoyed by a broad audience. I assume no professional training or background in these topics. In other words, even if you have no background in Christianity, the Israel-Palestine Conflict, or Middle Eastern history, you will still benefit from and enjoy reading this book. That said, I have also included historical, cultural, and theological insights that will appeal to professionally trained individuals and those with more experience. There is something for everyone here.

The second thing I should note is that the Bible—from Genesis to Revelation—is a Hebrew book reflecting a Middle Eastern worldview. If we wish to look at any passage of scripture in context, that context must be the context of the Holyland. The Middle Eastern perspective is a great way to begin studying and understanding scripture.

Throughout the book, I present the Middle Eastern roots of the Bible, exploring both customs and language to help you understand the Scripture more in-depth. Understanding first-century culture and ways of life will help clarify, confirm, and even sometimes correct your understanding of the Scriptures. I hope your faith is strengthened and you begin to see things from Jesus' viewpoint.

INTRODUCTION:

Third, this may be obvious, but I still need to say it—Jesus did not speak English. The common languages of the land in the first century were Aramaic, Greek, and some Hebrew. Jesus spoke all three. Yes, He lived in a land ruled by the Roman Empire; but He thought, lived, and died as a Middle Easterner. Likewise, Christians in the Middle East originally spoke Aramaic, just like Jesus.

When the church was born shortly after Jesus' ascent to heaven, the evangelist Luke mentions several different ethnic groups that were present and received the Holy Spirit. Arabs were among them (Acts 2:11). Those people from Arabia (The Aramean Christians) were present at the first feast of Pentecost. Thus, the Aramean Christians were some of the first Christians among the first groups to follow Jesus, and they have persisted in faithfulness to Christ throughout the centuries. The Arab Christians today see this momentous event as the origin of our faith in Christ as a community.

My point here is that there are long historical ties between Jesus and Arabs. Yes, some things have been complicated by Islam—and I discuss some of these challenges in subsequent chapters—but those complications have not severed the link between Jesus and his Arab followers. Few people, for example, are aware of the existence of more than ten million Arabic-speaking Christians who possess a rich heritage of both ancient and modern cultures. They have a lot to teach us.

Finally, when I use the word Christian in this book, I do not restrict my understanding to a single denomination. The term includes all the churches that believe in the whole Bible (both the Old and New Testament) and other common doctrinal beliefs, such as the Trinity of the Father, the Son, and the Holy Spirit. These beliefs unite the Christian world. They transcend human divisions and labels we give

Introduction:

to different groups, such as Catholics, Greek Orthodox, and Protestant churches.

The book is divided into three main sections with ten chapters:

In section one, I introduce the hidden bridge. I begin by explaining how to read the Bible through Jesus' eyes. I outline how history, geography, and theology come together in the person of Jesus and how understanding his way is the foundation of the bridge. In chapter one I start with Jesus as the foundation of the bridge, and in chapter two, I discuss the sources of the division of the bridge, and how Arabs and Jews came to be in such a protracted conflict in the Holyland. I also discuss some of the history of the Arab Christian faith and the modern history of the land that led up to important events throughout Israel's journey to modern times. This concludes section one.

Section two explores the various parts of the hidden bridge. I have organized chapters three through six geographically. I did this because the modern conflict has created vastly different experiences for Christians according to where they live. The experiences of Arab Christians in Israel are very different from those in the West Bank, Gaza, and Jerusalem. In each of these chapters, I relate biblical history and geography to the contemporary experiences of Christians and offer personal reflections. I finish this section with chapter seven on Muslim Background Believers and the Messianic Jewish community in chapter eight.

I have learned over the years that anyone who follows Jesus is an important part of the hidden bridge—this includes people who follow Jesus from Muslim and Jewish backgrounds. These two chapters have some background and history for how these groups came to faith, biblical insights, and personal accounts of my interactions with them.

INTRODUCTION:

Finally, in section three, I discuss how the hidden bridge is being revealed. In this Chapter, chapter nine, I briefly introduce the Christian Arab theology and how the development of this field has helped Palestinian Christians live faithfully to Christ despite the many challenges they face. And in the last chapter, chapter ten I delve into the parable of the good Samaritan. I conclude the book with the epilogue by offering several suggestions for how you might support and encourage Christians in the Holyland.

I pray that the Lord will bring clarity to our minds and give us more knowledge and understanding to strengthen and deepen our faith. I am praying that God will open our hearts to know the truth, His only truth, that can set us free. May we grow in God's wisdom to become better witnesses of the Gospel and to live out His victorious plan for our lives. May we advance His Kingdom in this exciting century that we live in.

Part One
Discovering the Hidden Bridge

Chapter 1. Jesus-The Foundation

Chapter 2. Sources of the Divide-Historical Background

Part One

The ancient Path leading to the Hidden Bridge

Chapter 1

Jesus—The Foundation

Jesus is the foundation of the bridge. Walking through the wilderness with your eyes aligned to the ancient paths, you can find life as you make your way toward him. But who was Jesus of Nazareth? What were the historical and geographical contexts in which he lived? How can we access them today? This chapter is about understanding Jesus' life and ministry from a Middle Eastern perspective. It's about discovering the ancient path.

Understanding the Bible Stories

Time has separated us from Jesus by thousands of years. But understanding culture and heritage can reconnect us to Him. The disconnect is partly due to the lack of information we have about people's beliefs of Jesus' time compared to our current contemporary circumstances.

In 2016, I visited the United States for the first time. I was able to go to a baseball game in New York at Yankee Stadium. But baseball can be boring if you don't know the rules like me. The game is just slow by nature. I noticed that event facilitators made it enjoyable by giving breaks occasionally, singing the national anthem, and doing random, silly things.

One thing they did was show replays from different angles on big screens, allowing the spectators to see the action from other points of view. They did this most when an umpire's call was challenged. These replays not only helped the umpires make the correct call, but they also helped me understand the game. Frankly, I wished it was football season when I visited. American football that is. I would have loved to see very large (allegedly intelligent) men smashing into each other. But I digress.

When Christians look at a biblical text today, they typically look at it from a Greco-Roman-Western worldview that has dominated the church for many centuries. That is good in some respects—you can only use the eyes God gave you. But it is only one point of view.

You need to bring your Western perspective, and you need to learn the Middle Eastern point of view, too. Having both systems will genuinely help you understand scripture. The two viewpoints—Western and Middle Eastern—can and should coexist. Nowadays, you can have both a Windows PC and a Mac computer. Having both can help you do a better job.

Let's situate Jesus in His authentic historical, sociological, and geographical context. The world was different in Jesus' day. There were other languages and different cultures. Those who were listening to Jesus at that time certainly understood His words. Specific details would have been familiar to his audience that helped them understand. As such, the scriptures are replete with tangible and local details of daily life in the first century Israel: place names, occupations, dwellings, religious rituals, and daily practices.

Jesus—The Foundation

Jesus spoke in terms that were easily comprehensible to His audience: rural Jews in first-century Galilee. Today, those details are not self-evident to those of us who live two thousand years removed. Ancient readers of the Gospels understood these local references, but modern readers usually do not.

When you translate the Bible from its original language into another, you lose much of its original meaning. And language is so important because it reflects the culture of its period. Take the Hebrew and Greek roots of Jesus' name, for example: Jesus or *"Iesous"* (Yay-soos) is the Greek equivalent of the Hebrew Joshua, meaning (the Lord is our salvation). *"Yeshua'"*, which is the shorter form of *"Yehoshua"* (Joshua), means (Yahweh is salvation). It was a common male Jewish name.

Since meaning is often lost in translation, I include explanations of key terms and concepts from their original languages because language is a rich way to develop and enrich your understanding of Jesus and his message.

I will also give examples that show how, throughout history, God has used the little to make the big, the common to make the uncommon, and the natural to make the supernatural. In these cases, it is essential to understand that the majority of the writers of the Bible lived in the Holyland, seeped in the cultures of their times. Otherwise, the author's intent to draw out these contrasts will be lost.

One important point to make here at the beginning is that the Bible and the land go together. Seeing the land with your eyes makes a big difference in your understanding of the Bible. Another reason you should visit the land of the Bible is to meet the indigenous Christians to interact with the people who understand the culture and history. This will make a difference. But I'm getting ahead of myself. I'll pick up the theme of local Christians in later chapters.

Another foundational point is this: the Bible is not a book of philosophy or fairytales. Instead, it records divine intervention in space and time in real places. Often, we can work out where these places are, which is exciting. But there are always three critical lines of evidence to consider when trying to identify and understand biblical locations:

- Geographical features in the landscape that match clues in the Bible.
- History, archaeology, and tradition—where early Christians believed events occurred.
- Theology of how God works through His creation, through nature, and through humanity.

When these three lines of evidence agree, we can be sure where the event happened in that place. This is the case for many of the events of Jesus' ministry in His land. This is a critical step to recovering the voice of Jesus, hearing Him in His own culture and on His own land. This is the only way to build a future based on this heritage.

Once we've identified the right (or most plausible) location, our task then becomes trying to understand the stories and metaphors that Jesus used. We must ask ourselves: What did his words mean to those who shared their culture and language with him? The Bible is not simply the Word of God for Christians in an abstract sense. Instead, it is the Word of God spoken through people in history. Those people and that history cannot be ignored. We must work to understand them.

In the Middle East, history, religion, and culture are interconnected. The West does not connect things this way or emphasize it. As a result, westerners don't often read or see the whole map. Think of it like watching a black-and-white TV instead of one in full-color 4K

HD. Jesus was and is not a cool blond-haired, blue-eyed homeboy dude! In the Middle East, we see Jesus in His real image, focusing not only on His divinity but on his humanity as well.

This different viewpoint allows us to understand more the historical Jesus so that we may understand the spiritual Jesus better. We look to understand the physical first because that connects us to the spiritual. God entered our world so we can enter His world.

Now, I'd like to shift from abstractly discussing these things and give two practical examples that illustrate how understanding Middle Eastern history, culture, and language lead to new biblical insights.

Jesus Second Hometown (Capernaum)

First, why did Jesus choose Capernaum as the base for His ministry when his hometown was Nazareth? The answer makes sense when you understand how social, cultural, and political backgrounds worked in the first century.

Capernaum was an extremely prosperous and vital city, especially in the period of Jesus. An important road once passed not far from the city, and trading caravans made their way to the city as a priority. It was thus a border city between the territories of Herod Antipas and Herod Phillip.

The founder of this city was a person named Nahum, and the village was known by his name, Nahum. The three root letters of this word are N-H-M in Hebrew which means comfort, so the literal meaning of the name Capernaum "*Kfar Nahum*" is this: "*Kfar*" means a village, and "*Nahum*" is a Hebrew root word that means comfort. So, Capernaum means the 'village of comfort.' We will discover together why it was such a comfortable middle class village to live in?

Chapter 1

In Jesus' day, Capernaum had around three thousand residents (not two or three hundred as some of the other villages nearby). It was considered the largest fishing village around the lake and had the largest synagogue. It was more of a middle-class village at the time. My point is that Capernaum was not simply a poor fishing village.

The city not only had a thriving fishing industry, but it also had millstones of various sizes manufactured for grinding wheat and pressing olives that were exported all over the country. Made of basalt stone (volcanic rock), these grinding mills were hard to shape and were perfect for the job. Not something you would find in a middle-of-no-were village.

Also, the area around Capernaum was very fertile, allowing farmers to easily grow crops, especially wheat and barley, from which flour and bread were made. Capernaum was the economic hub of the whole area with fishermen, farmers, and merchants.

Most people arrived at Capernaum by boat. The easiest journey, for example, from Nazareth was to walk to Magdala and then take a boat to Capernaum across the northern shore of the Sea of Galilee. Choosing Capernaum as His headquarters was strategic for Jesus. If Jesus had not made this important move from Nazareth, the backwoods village, hardly anyone would have heard about him.

Moreover, Jesus quickly made acquaintances with men in high places in Capernaum. Read the miracle found in (John 4:46-54). Jesus healed a nobleman's son. Some believe this nobleman ran Capernaum's fish market, overseeing the scales' weights and measures. He would likely protect Jesus when the need arose, covering for Jesus and not reporting him to Herod Antipas since Jesus had healed his son. Capernaum was an appealing home base.

Another miracle took place when Jesus raised to life the daughter of Jairus, the synagogue ruler of the city (Matthew 9:18-26). We don't know the little girl's name, only that she was 12 years old when she died. Everybody mocked Jesus when he claimed that she was sleeping. But the fear of God came upon them after Jesus raised her from the dead. After that, Jairus would undoubtedly have been sympathetic to Jesus. And since he was a powerful man in the city, he would have helped protect Jesus from the Sanhedrin courts. Jesus, therefore, had religious protection as well.

In (Luke 7:1-10), an unnamed centurion, sends word to Jesus that his servant is sick. The man had such faith that he asked Jesus to merely speak words of healing, and he believed his servant would be healed. Jesus did so and healed the servant. The centurion was a good Gentile man who had helped build the local synagogue. So here, a Roman soldier in charge of security, who likely lived in a Roman camp outside the city, would be able to provide some measure of protection for Jesus from the Roman legions. Jesus was, therefore, politically protected too.

In short, Jesus had social status, religious and political protection in Capernaum. These few examples illustrate how Jesus could freely teach and preach for two to three years without getting in trouble with the different authorities. God gave Jesus favor in the eyes of the inhabitants of Capernaum, a freedom he did not have in other cities, particularly in Jerusalem.

Jesus spent much of His time teaching in the hills above Capernaum where there was a triangle of cities. That triangle is known by Christian scholars as the Gospel triangle. And Jesus warned them, saying, "Woe to you, Beit Saida. Woe to you Capernaum. Woe to you, Korazim."

Chapter 1

The prophets taught that to whom much light was given, much responsibility was expected. Jesus gave more instruction to those three villages than anywhere else and thus expected more from them. He warned them that their hearts were hard and dark like the volcanic basalt rocks that spread in the Galilee and are indigenous to the area.

Jesus compared these three cities to the pagan cities of Tyre and Sidon. He even went so far as to say that their people would have believed if He had done these miracles in those non-Jewish cities. But the inhabitants of the Gospel triangle largely did not accept Jesus and hardened their hearts, much like the basalt rock everywhere around them.

Even though Jesus spent so much time there, the people of Capernaum were satisfied. They did not feel they needed the Lord. They were well established, having everything. We, as Christians, often choose to harden our hearts despite experiencing the work of God in our lives. This is why the Lord doesn't do more through us. Like the black basalt stones, our hearts can be hardened despite the miracles God has shown us.

It's astounding to realize that the people living in Capernaum and the surrounding areas hardened their hearts and did not believe in Christ even though they witnessed two-thirds of His miracles! May this open our hearts to His work in our lives and the lives of others around us.

The Capernaum example at the beginning of Jesus' ministry helps us see the importance of understanding history and geography. Let's go to the opposite end of Jesus' ministry to illustrate how his parables contain profound theology.

Jesus used parables to make profound points to his immediate listeners. And their meaning was clear. This made Him like other

Hebrew prophets who often took things from the environment as the symbolic basis for their messages.

Sometimes today, however, when we hear Jesus' parables, we give them a different significance than what Jesus intended. Our understanding is disconnected from time, space, and how people thought that day. That is why we must work to understand the parables in their historical and cultural contexts.

Jesus used images to enrich our understanding of God beyond time and space. An examination of Jesus' language and cultural contexts reveals him to be an astute theologian. If for Jesus, stories and dramatic actions were the language of theology, then the culture of the storyteller is crucial.

Chapter 1

Capernaum left in Ruins

The Daughters of Jerusalem

Let's look at the smallest parable in the Bible, one that is frequently misunderstood today without a proper understanding of the background of the first century culture. It has profound meaning despite its brevity. Jesus' last parable was only two lines, and it was given on His way to the cross, almost midway from the condemnation to the crucifixion.

Jesus said in (Luke 23:31), "For if they do these things in a green tree, what shall be done in the dry?" Jesus was speaking to the daughters of Jerusalem, who were weeping because of what the Romans were doing to Jesus. Jesus was saying that if this is what they do to those whose teachings are green, what would happen in Jerusalem when it gets dry-wood preachers? Here's the key: the Zealots, the radical anti-Romans, had two nicknames, thieves and dry wood.

Thieves were never crucified at this time, so the two people who hung next to Jesus were rebels who revolted against the Roman Empire. But they also became thieves in the eyes of the Romans because they stole from those traveling between cities. During their attacks against the Romans, the Zealots would also collect dry wood, mix it with oil, burning it, then throw it on the Roman soldiers before running away. This is how the war got started.

You can't quickly start a fire with green wood; it does not burn as easily as dry wood. And the rebels would use dry wood in their rebellions against the Romans. Jesus was being faithful by not returning evil for evil. Jesus sought to bring peace and love, but no one could understand His message. Jesus had compassion for those that wept and told them not to cry for Him but to weep for themselves because a war was coming soon. The inhabitants of Jerusalem would be among the first casualties.

Chapter 1

In Hebrew, "daughters" is the word "*Banote.*" But when Hebrew uses the word daughters in connection with a place or thing, it has an entirely different meaning. So, "daughters of Jerusalem" means the poor outside the wall. In Hebrew, a municipality or city is a feminine word. A walled city is known as a mother to the poor around it. Those outside the city walls were also called daughters.

Therefore, the terms daughters of Israel, daughters of Judea, daughters of Jerusalem, and daughters of my people would have been understood to include the old and young, males and females outside the city wall. There are many places in the Bible where the word, daughters means, the poor, the unprotected ones.

Now, what were the daughters of Jerusalem doing? They were crying. As Jesus left Jerusalem carrying the cross, the text says, "But Jesus turning unto them said, Daughters of Jerusalem, weep not for me, but weep for yourselves, and for your children" (Luke 23:28).

As such, the daughters of Jerusalem were the poor people outside the city wall, old and young, men and women, who were weeping that Friday afternoon. A war would be coming very soon, and the poor people would be killed outside the walled city of Jerusalem. Jesus told them to weep for themselves and not for Him. Even in His agony, Jesus had compassion on them. In other words, if the people thought Jesus' crucifixion was bad, they should wait until the war started! At the time, you did not need to be a prophet (no disrespect to Jesus) to know a war with Rome was coming, and it would be fierce.

Are you beginning to see how appreciating the text's historical, linguistic, and cultural background can enrich your Biblical understanding? Jesus was thoroughly Middle Eastern. And he was entirely Jewish. *"Yeshua"* was his Hebrew name. He taught as a rabbi, learned with sages, and taught in the Hebrew language. He was born to a Jewish mother, lived, and was raised in a Jewish home that observed the Torah. He began His ministry in a Jewish way at the age of 30. He engaged in a thoroughly Jewish ministry, even raising up disciples as a rabbi would. And He died a Jew.

Jesus was a child of this land. This is what unites Jesus with the people of the land. But at the same time, He exceeded His Jewishness. He went beyond it and gave us a new vision. He was more open and more inclusive. He invited all. He asked all to follow Him.

John the Baptizer was not Baptist. Mary, Jesus' mother, was not Catholic. Jesus was not a Christian. Jesus, his companions, and his family were all Jewish from this area, land, and culture. Jesus was a Palestinian Jew! Before you get upset because I called Jesus Palestinian, let me explain. The name Palestine was used over the centuries to describe what today is known as the Holyland. People who lived in historical Palestine are called Palestinians. And historically, Jesus belonged to this area of the world. That makes Jesus a Palestinian Jew! Don't worry. I will explain this more in the next chapter.

The Rich Heritage and Culture of Middle Eastern Christianity

Although the geographic center of Christianity may have shifted to the West from its origin, Jesus still came from the Holyland. His culture was Middle Eastern. He spoke Semitic languages, which were and are from the Middle East. Christians in the Middle East today have a unique lens for understanding the teachings of Jesus and interpreting the Gospels. They have faithfully remained in the land, preserving essential aspects of his teaching and legacy. We have a shared culture and languages with Jesus.

Chapter 1

The more than ten million Arabic-speaking Christians live in the Middle East trace their origins to the day of Pentecost as they heard Peter's preaching. Peter specifically told them to go from Jerusalem throughout Judea and Samaria and to the rest of the places and share the good news.

Arabic-speaking Christianity is known to have been widespread, and centuries of high-quality Arabic Christians have shared their faith in Middle Eastern cultures. They are ethnically closer to the Semitic world of Jesus than the Greek and Latin cultures of the West.

These Middle Eastern churches have lived as a minority for thousands of years, especially during times of persecution. Such troubles and struggles are not new. Our ancestors have kept their faith for over 2,000 years through these same issues. A diamond ring is admired and worn with pride, but with time, it needs to be taken to a jeweler to be cleaned to restore its original brilliance. The time is now to start to appreciate more the Christians of the Holyland, this diamond to be polished to start shinning after being neglected for all of the past centuries.

In the West, the term Arab is often equated with Muslim. This is certainly a misconception of both Middle Eastern history and Christianity. Arab Christians are neither an invention nor a Western product. Arab Christians today are part of the Arab civilization and culture.

For example, centuries of high-quality Arabic Christian literature remain, for the most part, unpublished and unknown. All these language sources, Syriac (a sister language to Aramaic), Hebrew, Aramaic, and Arabic, share the broader culture of the ancient Middle East.

Arabic-speaking Christianity was known to have become widespread. And it even made its way to the Arabian Peninsula and elsewhere through trade. However, with the rise of Islam, Arabic gradually became the primary theological language for all Eastern Christians. Everyone started to speak more Arabic than Aramaic from the seventh century and onwards.

That said, the Bible is full of references to customs and traditions that continue to exist in modern-day Arab Christian life. For one, The Christian Arabs of the Holyland have been credited with preserving the indigenous Semitic place names for many sites mentioned in the Bible. We know where many biblical sites are, we have preserved their names and kept the local indigenous traditions.

We can also use dance as an example. The most famous Arab dance is called *"Dabke."* The dance is marked by synchronized jumping, stamping, and movement. It's somewhat similar to tap dancing. One version is performed by men, another by women. Yet this dance has been performed by Middle Eastern villagers since ancient Canaanite and Phoenician times to celebrate feast days.

To get a deeper understanding of the cultural connections, let's examine the differences in the manner of speaking between people from the Middle East versus Westerners. The normal and daily conversations of Arab Christians are full of biblical language and atmosphere.

One of these traditional ways of thinking and speaking is the benediction of 'God bless your hands' or *"Yeslamou Edek"* in Arabic. This is how we thank a person for their hard work and preparation. It is much more meaningful than the simple 'thank you' you receive in the West.

Similarly, we find many blessings and praises in the Bible. Here's another example: We thank God not only before we start eating but also after we finish. We say Praise God or *"Alhamdu Lellah"* in Arabic. Appreciating God for what He gave us to eat and not forgetting His blessings after we are full and have already enjoyed His provision.

Before the development of the Arabic alphabet, the Aramaic alphabet was the common language used by ancient Arab tribal groups in the Levant. Eventually, the culture was Arabized, especially during the beginning of Islam in the seventh century as I mentioned earlier.

In Arabic today, there are a lot of Aramaic words that we still use. Interestingly enough, the more north you live in the Middle East, such as in the Aramaic communities in Lebanon, Syria, and Iraq, the more you notice Aramaic showing up in daily Arabic exchanges. The more south you go, toward the desert, the Aramaic words are used less where the Arabic language is stronger.

Let me give you another quick example of this difference in Middle Eastern cultures. When we say, Good Morning to someone, all the locals in the land answer the same, regardless of Jews, Christians or Muslims, "The morning of the light."

These are small things, but understanding language is vital to understanding culture. There is a rich meaning behind the way we answer whether in Arabic or Hebrew as both have the same Semitic origins. Good Morning in Arabic is *"Sabah Elkhair."* We answer, (the morning of the light) or *"Sabah Elnour."* In Arabic, *"Elnour"* means, the light. It is the same in Hebrew. We say, *"Boker Tov"* or Good Morning. The way it is answered is *"Boker Or,"* which means, "the morning of the light."

There are three reasons we respond this way. When the sun comes up, darkness immediately flees, and you can see better. You would know your bearings and where to go since you can see the path. Thus:

1. The light from the sun gives first direction and guidance.
2. The light from the sun brings joy and encouragement for the new day is fresh and open.
3. The light of the sun brings purification and sanctification.

The sun is the light of the physical world, whereas Jesus is the light of the spiritual world. He is the light that, in a general sense, enlightens the human conscience and thereby makes all humanity responsible before God.

The Christian's joy is in knowing that light is not only greater than darkness but also outlasts the darkness. So, we should reflect this light as the true light that comes from Jesus Christ, the source of God's light. And as the sun is the source of light, whether it is daytime or nighttime, so is the Son of God, our spiritual light in dark times and good times. Both always shine. Even when it is dark outside, and we can't see the sun, it still shines somewhere else on earth.

To take this to a higher level, consider oil lamps used in biblical times. We Middle Eastern Christians represent the clay pottery of the lamp, holding the oil, which is the Holy Spirit's anointing. Our lamp should be full all the time, but if the clay pot is cracked, we will lose the oil, and thus we struggle. The wick is the soul, the connector between the body and the Holy Spirit that constantly produces light, which is not easy. However, the more the wick (the soul) is dipped in the oil (the Holy Spirit), the more we can show light in this dark world.

Again, we are the clay vessels; the wick is the soul dipped in the oil to fill us with the Holy Spirit. The wick goes through the mouth, and the oil flows through the wick, filled with the Spirit and fire to be His light and witness. We must dip our hearts and ignite our mouths to speak out so that we may shine. You are a clay vessel, and you have the treasure of the Spirit of God within you so that you can release God's light through you.

Burning the wick is like burning the soul, but the more the wick is dipped in the oil of the Holy Spirit, the easier it will burn! Wow! Think about it. The clay is nothing…just dirt and dust. We are a soul dipped and anointed with the Holy Spirit. The value is not the container. What is *inside* the container is what matters. What is inside us should reflect His light, and a little light can overcome all the darkness easily, for darkness can't stand against even the smallest light.

Therefore, the lamp is the body, and the oil is the Holy Spirit, and the wick the soul, the link between the body and spirit. We are a soul in a body, not a body in the soul. We reflect the light only; Jesus is the source. The power is from Him, not from us. Our clay bodies are very fragile and easy to break. We are weak compared to the power inside us, the oil of the Holy Spirit.

The oil of the Spirit was poured out on Pentecost. The oil of the Spirit goes into our soul and ignites it, filling our spirit with light. In (Acts 2:4), with the birth of the church in Jerusalem, there were flames of fire when the people were filled with the Spirit. Our oil lamps are set alight and ignited in the baptism of the Spirit. We have the source of Light of life within us as followers of the true source of Light, Jesus Christ, our Anointed Savior.

We practice our faith through our lives, thinking of others and giving to the needy. We don't give people our leftovers or extras, but we offer the freshest and best of our food to others. We serve our neighbors and the needy first. After that, we eat the leftovers. This is for community our well-being, and it is what our parents have taught us. We live in communities, and this matters most to us—the well-being of our community. It is more important than our individual well-being.

All that makes us more successful than we would otherwise be, acting as individuals. When you go alone, you can go very fast. But moving together with a community means you can go far. When we reach a goal together, everyone celebrates the success.

The key is the personal touch. Middle Eastern culture is based on relationships, storytelling, and people spending a long time with one another. People in Eastern cultures are not so worried about schedules and quotas or sales figures, returning e-mails or phone calls quickly. They are interested in personal contact.

How does this eastern heritage and culture matter? The West (Greco-Roman) versus the East (Aramaic- Hebraic) have different ways of thinking. The Greek mind is analytical, linear, and abstract. The Middle Eastern mind is more visual and focused on imagery. In a Middle Eastern view, for example, we see God as a steadfast rock, while the West views God as omnipotent.

Middle Eastern culture handles things differently than Western culture does. When you ask a question of an elder, instead of giving a straight answer, he will reply with a story. The story is the answer; an answer seeped in that person's experience, history, and culture. This has helped me understand the parables of Jesus. This type of response is still common in my culture.

Jesus, the human being, lived in the Holyland. His culture is of our Middle Eastern culture. To recover our authentic Christian heritage, we must acknowledge and affirm the Jewishness of Jesus and of His early followers in the proper context with their own customs. He spoke from this culture, and we, Christians of the Holyland, are closer to this culture than others outside it.

Chapter 1

Understanding Jesus in his first-century context helps the twenty-first-century disciples of Jesus live a victorious Christian life today.

The truth is that if you wish to know the true God of the whole world, you must look in the face of Jesus. He is God in human form, the foundation of the hidden bridge.

Oil Lamp

Chapter 2

Sources of the Divide— Historical Background

Before we can appreciate how Christians of the Holyland are the hidden bridge, we need to understand the sources of the divide, the things that have caused the divisions between Arabs and Jews. How did such a great valley come to separate them in the first place? And then how did the bridge come to be hidden? The one-word answer to these questions is history.

In this chapter, we will look at the modern history of the land. We will focus primarily on the past 100 years. This may be a small window of time when contemplating the whole history of the Holyland, but this period is essential because it's when the divisions began.

The current divisions are not eternal or inevitable as many people suppose. I often hear tourists say things like, "They have been fighting for thousands of years...," and it pains me every time. First, it is simply untrue, and second, it comes across as dismissive of the Christian calling to be peacemakers. It sounds like the person is saying, 'why bother?' If that attitude is their starting point, peace is impossible.

That said, I encourage you to approach the coming pages with an open mind. I give a bird's eye view of the key events, covering only the highlights. If you enjoy history, this will be your favorite chapter. If history is not your thing, I try not to overwhelm you with details. If you get bogged down, feel free to skip to the final section, where I summarize the five key issues that make up the present impasse. That's enough to keep you oriented moving forward.

The important thing to say first is that these events have led to the situation we are dealing with in our modern period, whether bad or good. We cannot separate our lives from them. Today's reality is defined by the past. Christians have found themselves in the middle of this conflict, and we have done our best to be faithful to Jesus and his teachings. To be the hidden bridge, we need to understand the conflict from both sides. We must be pro-Palestinian and pro-Israeli. We want both sides to make peace.

This is a challenging position sometimes because everyone wants to know what side you are on, and what side you take. But as Christians, we need to take a larger view. We must faithfully live our calling as the hidden bridge.

Sources of the Divide—Historical Background

INTRODUCTION

The conflict found in Israel is not an ancient conflict as so many people think. In the southern part of the Ottoman Empire, Arab Jews, Arab Christians, and Arab Moslems about 100 to 120 years ago lived all together in the region of Southern Syria under the Ottoman Empire. The land of Palestine back then was part of a larger region that included present day Jordan, Syria, and Lebanon (all of which together were called Bilad El-sham).

They were not fighting each other. The Middle East was generally a peaceful place whereas wars were found more often in Europe and other countries at that time.

Since Arabs and Jews coexisted in peace for many centuries, there is no reason on earth—no historical reason, at least—why they should not continue to live as good neighbors in the future. Please know that the Arabs were never the enemies of the Jews. On the contrary, they were the ones who accepted them back throughout history when they were suffering in many parts of the West.

The Ottoman Turks ruled this land for almost 400 years. A good place to start if we want to understand about how the Arab-Israeli conflict developed is the end of the 19th century and the beginning of the 20th century. The land of Palestine remained under various Islamic rulers from the middle 7th century until the fall of the Ottoman Turks in 1917. It was a Moslem world that was very much dictated. As the Moslem Arab population grew through these centuries, religious leaders turned churches into mosques, imposed oppressive taxes on Christians and Jews, established Islam as the official religion, and decreed Arabic to be the common language.

Chapter 2

While the Turks were ruling, they maintained peace among these various communities and allowed rabbis to rule the Jews, priests to govern the Christians, and Qadis to judge the Muslims. Under the Turkish Empire, the people of the land lived together in peace. At the time, 3% were Jewish around 15,000, 10% were Christians, around 50,000, and 87% were Moslems, around 435,000. The total population of the land back then was almost 500,000. Many Jews living in the land also considered themselves locals, spoke Arabic and identified with the people in other numerous ways. Indigenous Jews, before Zionism, were also Arabs as that was their culture and language.

But the 19th and 20th centuries were an age of religious explosion, an age of political invention, an age of growing freedom, of trade, and of urbanization. The fruit of the land began to be exported internationally. The printing press brought enlightenment, independent thought, freedom of expression, and opportunity to break away from constraint. It was the beginning of productization.

All the world's horizons were being expanded so that the center of power grew. It was the beginning of the steam power and industrial production. The world began to change and transportation via ship and train connected cultures and civilizations like never before throughout the Turkish empire.

Thus, modernization started to invade. The 19th and the 20th centuries were a turning point in the history of the Holyland. Moreover, because of its strategic location, political powers began turning their eyes upon the land, particularly in Europe as the world opened more and more.

The society of the Holyland in those centuries was made up of mosaic groups, Jews, Christians, and Muslims. The Ottoman state, as a successor to Islamic political development recognized the autonomous state of all non-Muslim religious sects in a millet system. The Christians, for example, lived under the protection of the Sultan, paying tribute for this trust. In return, the state protected their lives and property.

One of the negative aspects of the Millet system was exploitation, as the Ottoman Empire began collapsing. The intervention of imperialist countries—France, England, and Russia—in declaring their protection for the different religious sects was only a pretext for intervention in the internal affairs of the Ottoman Empire, helping it to slowly get weaker and weaker until it got sick and died!

The British Mandate, 1917—1947

In 1917, in the broader context of World War I, the Allied forces, led by British General Edmund Allenby, entered Jerusalem after the surrender of the Ottoman forces. Britain became the occupying power of Palestine and would rule the land for the next 30 years.

Theodor Herzl perpetuated a common myth: "A land without a people for a people without a land." This gave the impression that the land was empty, ready to be inhabited. This was not the case. Before the Jews came, the land was inhabited primarily by Arabs. The Jews only represented ten percent of the population at that time living only in big cities such as Jerusalem and Tiberias.

The Balfour Declaration

Christian Zionism had deep roots in Britain, particularly among the British leadership. Their desire to establish a Jewish state in Palestine was behind Britain's quick issuing of the Balfour Declaration in 1917.

Chapter 2

The Zionist movement managed to convince the Jews to leave where they were living and move to the Promised Land. To support this, the British government decided to endorse the establishment of a Jewish home in Palestine. After discussions within the cabinet and consultations with Jewish leaders, the decision was made public in a letter. British Foreign Secretary Sir Arthur James Balfour conveyed in a letter to Baron Lionel Walter Rothschild a declaration approved by the British Cabinet. The contents of this letter became known as the Balfour Declaration.

I want to make two crucial points about the text. First, the Balfour Declaration pledged British support for the establishment of a Jewish national home in Palestine. Under the patronage of British power, the Jews would be able to develop and set up the administrative machinery that would enable the implementation of Zionist objectives. This declaration was the golden key that unlocked the door for Jews to come to Palestine. An imperialist country granted land to displaced Jews that it had no right to give. Think of it this way: one nation (Britain) solemnly promised a second nation (Israel), the country of a third nation (Palestine).

Second, notice that the declaration calls the land Palestine. Palestine was a geographical term for all the land, and it applied to all the land's residents: Palestinian Jews, Palestinian Muslims, and Palestinian Christians. Undoubtedly, the Balfour Declaration was key in setting off the tragic conflict between Arabs and Zionists that would last until today.

So, whether you like the term Palestine or not, that was now the official historical name given to this land by the British. We also need to acknowledge that the British played a significant role in setting up the conflict. As a result of British rule and their support for Zionism, the 1920s witnessed the growth and expansion of Jewish administrative, religious, educational, cultural, and artistic institutions in the Holyland.

The land was the birthplace of the Jewish people. Here, their spiritual and national identity was formed. They revived their language and started to build cities. The land of Israel went from being a mere spiritual ideal to becoming a physical reality where Hebrew was restored as the holy tongue of the people.

Waves of Jewish immigration grew large enough to arouse Arab nationalism opposing Zionism. This, in turn, prompted the Jews to start forming defensive forces. So, in 1921, the Zionist paramilitary organization, *"Hagganah"*, the term means (defense), was formed secretly and illegally. The British turned a blind eye to their activities and gave the group its covert support.

Together, based on the decision of the 1920 San Remo Conference in Italy that was attended by the four principal allied powers of World War I (Britain, France, Italy, and Japan), a mandate to govern Syria and Lebanon was awarded to France. The British received a mandate for Palestine, Transjordan, and Mesopotamia (Iraq). The league of Nations Council ratified the decision in 1922 without the consent of the Palestinians.

The Mandate, thus, formally commenced in 1923, and Britain became the governing power in Palestine. By 1925, the Palestinians were stripped of Ottoman citizenship. Their Palestinian nationality was issued the same year.

In 1928, during Yom Kippur, Jews tried to set up benches at the Western Wall. This caused riots, and the British intervened to break them up. Arab nationalism was aroused, and opposition to Zionism spread rapidly. This nationalism quickly became violent with a call for political unity against Zionism and the British imperial authorities. In 1929, the "*Hagganah*" obtained official recognition. The organization later grew into the central defense mechanism of the Zionist movement. Militarism became a value in creating Jewish pride and power.

Foreign Office,
November 2nd, 1917.

Dear Lord Rothschild,

    I have much pleasure in conveying to you, on behalf of His Majesty's Government, the following declaration of sympathy with Jewish Zionist aspirations which has been submitted to, and approved by, the Cabinet

>His Majesty's Government view with favour the establishment in Palestine of a national home for the Jewish people, and will use their best endeavours to facilitate the achievement of this object, it being clearly understood that nothing shall be done which may prejudice the civil and religious rights of existing non-Jewish communities in Palestine, or the rights and political status enjoyed by Jews in any other country"

I should be grateful if you would bring this declaration to the knowledge of the Zionist Federation.

The Balfour Declaration

CHAPTER 2

Immigration and Land Exploitation

In the 1930s, America's doors began closing to new immigrants, and many Jews decided to come to Palestine instead. Those who came were largely middle-class businesspeople and artisans. The Arabs began to provide cheap labor as they were better farmers and more tied to the land. Their willingness to help only made younger Jews more arrogant, and they looked down upon such labor.

In 1935, the Jewish population doubled, and immigration and land sales surpassed all previous records. Arabs became increasingly afraid of a Jewish takeover. At the same time, instability in Greater Syria (now Lebanon, Palestine, Syria, and Jordan) played a significant role in escalating the outward immigration of Palestinians from their land.

As there was an increase in the awareness of Christian Arabs in Europe and the New World, this increased their desire to see those countries and emigrate to them to exploit the available economic opportunities in the region.

After the end of World War I, many Arabs decided to return to their birthplace, but the British authorities closed the doors to them. They did this while opening the doors wide for Jewish immigrants.

British policy allowed incoming Jewish immigrants to obtain citizenship under easy conditions while placing numerous obstacles in the face of native-born Palestinians who wanted to return. Due to this British policy, only 100 Palestinian applications were approved from 9,000 submitted by immigrants wishing to return to their mother country. Palestinian immigrants, deprived of their citizenship, faced challenging circumstances outside and inside their motherland.

Sources of the Divide—Historical Background

The Great Palestinian Revolt (1936–1939)

Between 1936 and 1939, Palestinian Arabs revolted against the Jewish immigrants. The revolt involved three years of organized activity that grew the Arab national movement. This marked the beginning of the three years of riots. The outbreak included a general strike of Arab workers and a boycott of Jewish products.

These actions swiftly escalated against the Jews and the British. They had several goals: to stop the sale of land to the Jews, to place a complete hold on Jewish immigration, and to establish an Arab government. As a result, the British forced the Arab leadership into exile. That created an Arab leadership vacuum in the region.

Palestinian revolutionists began wearing the *"Kufiyah"*, a head covering that hid their identities. But British authorities confronted anyone wearing it. In response, the commanders of the revolt called on Palestinians everywhere to stop wearing the Turkish *"tarboosh"*, the hat they typically wore, and instead don the *"Kufiyah"* in support of the revolution and prevent the British from chasing revolutionists.

While there had been cycles of violence earlier, Palestinian nationalism was aroused, and violent opposition to Zionism spread during the three-year revolt. It was directed initially at the Jews and later at the British. But despite the resistance, the Jewish population doubled, and more Jewish settlements were built to create facts on the ground.

The Arabs woke up to what was happening, but unfortunately, it was too late. Palestinians initially accepted the Jewish immigrants, not realizing that the Jews wanted to be in control. The Palestinian people at that time were simple and hospitable. They did not expect to have the land ripped away from them in such a short time or come home to find Jews, claiming that they had purchased their land.

When the Palestinians revolted, they first attacked the Jews living in Jaffa because the city symbolized Jewish immigration. It was the port from where most Jews arrived to the land. Arabs were angered by the injustices perpetrated by their British occupiers and by seeing their land overtaken by foreigners. That was unacceptable.

Was it right that the burden of solving the problem of the European Jewish Diaspora fell primarily on the shoulders of the Palestinians? Palestinians were not responsible for the historical suffering of the Jews in Europe. Foreigners were attempting to solve their own Jewish problem at the expense of the native inhabitants of Palestine. In the process, they helped create the crisis that has threatened world peace for over a century.

As a result of the revolt and after the Jewish population reached 450,000, the British government issued what was known as the White Paper in 1939 to clarify Britain's policy in Palestine. It placed restrictions on Jewish immigration and land purchases and envisioned an independent state in Palestine within ten years. It also restricted Jewish immigration to Palestine to 15,000 annually for five years, protecting Palestinian property rights from Zionist acquisition.

The paper revoked any intention to create a Jewish state. This infuriated the Zionists, who then organized terrorist groups and launched a bloody campaign against the British and the local Palestinians. They aimed to drive them both out of Palestine and thus pave the way for the establishment of the Zionist state.

The Second World War (1939–1945)

World War II erupted in 1939 and continued through 1945. The conflict was the most widespread war in history. It resulted in tens of millions of deaths and vast destruction in many countries, including

SOURCES OF THE DIVIDE—HISTORICAL BACKGROUND

using atomic bombs on Hiroshima and Nagasaki, Japan. The Holocaust was another horrific aspect of the war. After centuries of antisemitism and persecution, six million Jews were slaughtered under the Nazis in Germany. Jewish survivors, having nowhere else to go, came on boats to Palestine.

The British Mandate in Palestine struggled during the early part of the war. They let locals join their police forces and gain control over the region as they were focused on Hitler and Germany. Palestine was converted into a vast logistics base for the entire British army in the Middle East. As a result, camps were built, roads paved, and airfields were installed.

When the war ended, Palestine was the only country open to take the Jews. Therefore, the rise of Nazism in Germany in the 1930s, and the oppression of Jews in Europe, cultivated in the Holocaust during World War II, that led to increased Jewish immigration to Palestine.

But even during all this, there was the combination of the Jewish struggle for independence on the one hand, and the problem of the displaced survivors in Europe, who insisted on immigrating to Palestine, on the other. Jewish underground groups fought British rule in various ways, and some of the time jointly as part of the newly organized Hebrew resistance movements.

For Zionists, the liberation of the land became the prime objective by means of armed struggle against Britain. Zionist paramilitary organizations—the *"Hagganah"*, *"Irgun"*, and *"Stern"*, among others —escalated terrorist activities against Palestinian and British targets. In 1946, fighters for the freedom of Israel bombed the British headquarters at the King David Hotel. Additionally, the *"Hagganah"* destroyed ten major bridges leading into Palestine to restrict British movements. The attack became known as the Black Sabbath. And during that time, the Jews established eleven new settlements in the Negev desert in the southern part of the country.

The British responded by carrying out a major raid, jailing Jewish leaders and confiscating weapons and ammunition. The British also set up camps in Cyprus to detain Jewish immigrants trying to reach the land. In Palestine, the gradual decline of the British forces resulted in a more intense struggle between Jews and Arabs to control strategic points everywhere.

That period marked the end of religious Zionism and began the period of militant Zionism. In less than a decade, this spirit would bring about the establishment of the State of Israel. In 1946 Zionist Congress, the first after the Second World War, planned for the immediate establishment of the Jewish State. In 1947, Britain decided to terminate the Mandate and relinquished the question of Palestine to the United Nations.

The Mandate officially ended with the withdrawal of the British from Palestine. The British had promised independence for both Arabs and Jews, but everyone had become upset after almost thirty years of failure to keep that promise. In the end, the British had made enemies of both the Jews and the Palestinians.

The United Nations Partition Plan (1947)

In 1947, the British government announced that it intended to give up the Mandate and hand the Palestine problem to the United Nations (UN). The UN voted to create two separate states: a Jewish state which covered 55% of the land, and an Arab state which would be made up of the remaining 45% of the land. Jerusalem and the surrounding area would become an international zone.

The UN general assembly approved the Partition Plan by a vote of 33 to 13, with ten abstentions, largely through the influence of the United States. While the Jews in Palestine appeared to accept the plan initially, Palestinian Arabs rejected it outright. War broke out with both sides increasing their terrorist activities.

By 1947, the population of the land had grown to around 2 million people, with 30% Jews and 70% Palestinians (60% Muslims and 10% Christians). The Jews were concentrated in the cities, making them about 50% of the urban population. The countryside, however, was still about 90% Arab. That means the plan gave Jews 55% of the land while they were only 30% of the total population, while it gave 45% of the land to Palestinians, who made up 70% of the population.

Palestine was comprised of less than 10,000 square miles. Of this, the Arabs were to retain 4,300 square miles, while the Jews, who represented one-third of the population, were allotted 5,700 square miles. The Jews also got better land: they received the fertile coastal belt while the Arabs were to make do, for the most part, with the hills. The division was not equal. It clearly favored Zionists. The Arabs, of course, objected.

The Jews, on the other hand, celebrated. They had been facing persecution and death on a scale that amounted to genocide, and now they were being offered a state. They were ready to give up their aspiration for Jerusalem because a small home was better than no home. They were motivated to make a life-or-death attempt to create a state of their own, and this plan pointed toward its success.

Thus, overnight, the UN solemnly laid the foundations of a new moral order by which the Jews, the vast majority of whom had only been in Palestine 30 years or less, were deemed to have equal and even superior rights to those of the Palestinians who had lived there for centuries.

Chapter 2

The Palestinian Arabs, both Christians but predominantly Muslim, concluded that they were being required to pay for the antisemitic sins of the Christian West. For the Palestinians, it was a disaster. It was not fair that these strangers had come from other lands to take what had been theirs for centuries. Ultimately, the partition plan was never implemented and thrown into the garbage of history. It never succeeded. But it wasn't that simple.

This reminds me of the story of King Solomon's solution to cut the baby in half to determine whom the baby belonged to—for two women claimed the baby as their own. The true mother offered to allow the other woman to have the baby instead of killing and dividing her child. Thus, Solomon knew to whom the baby belonged. It belonged to the real mother who did not agree to cut her baby in half.

For Palestinians, there was no way this land division could be accepted. The land was their baby. It was unthinkable for Palestinians to agree to such a plan. This was the land they had lived in their whole lives. They felt it was wrong to divide or even give any portion of it away to someone else.

In the wake of the UN resolution to partition Palestine, the British decided not to implement it, declaring instead that they would finally leave Palestine. The following year, in 1948, the Jewish state was declared even before the last British flag was lowered.

The Zionists seized the opportunity to fill the power vacuum. For the first time in thousands of years, the Jews had a chance to reclaim their original homeland. They finally had a historic opportunity to create a state for themselves. It was the act of a people fighting for their future, a declaration of independence.

The State of Israel was declared at four in the afternoon on a Friday shortly before Shabbat. The declaration was made in the home of

Meir Dizengoff, the first mayor of Tel Aviv, who lived in a small apartment built on the roof of the building. The location was chosen because it was one of the most secure structures, with small windows. The ceremony was held in secret.

At Haifa Bay, the British commissioner Allan Cunningham saluted the lowering of the British flag, leaving an imbalance of power. An intense struggle broke out immediately between Jews and Arabs for more control of strategic points.

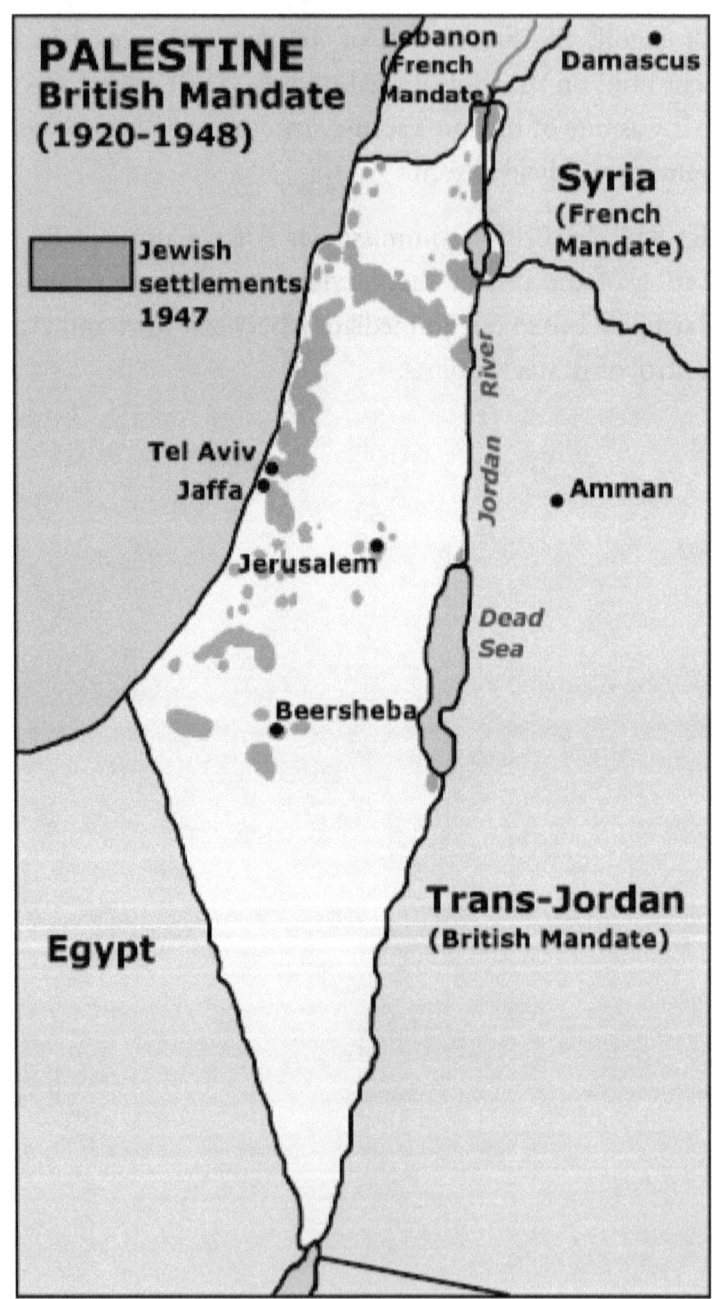

During the British Mandate

Sources of the Divide—Historical Background

The War of Israel's Independence and the Palestinian Catastrophe, 1948

The Israeli State is Born

Clashes immediately broke out between the Arabs and Zionists, soon becoming the 1948 war of independence. Initially, Arabs had a decisive advantage. At 600,000, the Jews were vastly outnumbered by the 1,500,000 Arabs. Plus, those who would soon join from Egypt 10,000 soldiers, Jordan 4,500, Syria 3,000, Lebanon 1,000, and Iraq 3,000. In all, joined with some 500 local Palestinian untrained fighters, that is close to a total of 22,000 Arab soldiers together with the neighboring Arab countries started to attack the fledgling Jewish state. The Arabs had superior manpower, weapons, training, and terrain control. The Israel defense was mostly weaponless and still coming to grips with their sudden freedom.

The Arabs thought they would succeed within weeks of their initial push. But they did not coordinate their efforts well and sometimes worked at odds with one another. Each army did whatever it wanted, with no clear consolidation of leadership. For example, the Egyptian army, the largest and most unorganized of the invading forces, was commanded by politicians rather than professional officers. They were supposed to thrust up the coast but were repulsed swiftly and successfully by the new Jewish state, which after that, counterattacked and managed to route the invaders on most battlefronts.

Even though the Jews were new to the Land and did not know the terrain well, sometimes going thirsty due to ignorance of nearby wells, they successfully turned back each army. They were much more organized and united than the five Arab armies fighting together.

Chapter 2

This does not mean Israel had it easy. The Jews found that the British, before leaving, had closed supply routes from the west. This caused shortages in their war efforts. The Arabs had come from the east and were not affected by these disruptions. Once the Jews reopened the supply routes, they could bring in more arms, ammunition, and other supplies that helped turn the tide against the fragmented and disorganized Arabs.

The Jews went on the offensive. They broke the siege of Jerusalem, where some of the war's heaviest fighting took place. They won the battle for the roads leading into the city, subdued the Palestinian Arabs, and gained control of a significant portion of the territory.

The first stage of their offensive was to provide safe passage to Jerusalem for their soldiers. This meant they had to destroy several villages on the route to clear the way. One village was called *"Deir Yassin"*. The Jews attacked its inhabitants and massacred more than one hundred Palestinians, including women, children, and the elderly. The attack led to a Palestinian exodus from the village.

In another instance, the Zionist paramilitary organizations perpetrated one of their most heinous massacres at *"Tantura"*, a village near the city of Haifa, killing nearly another 200 Palestinians. This massacre was not public knowledge until the year 2000. But the Palestinians always knew, and stories of such destruction spread terror among them, leading more to flee their homes.

In the end, the fledgling Jewish state won. For the Jews, this was their war of independence. One percent of the Jewish population, that is 6,000 Jewish men were killed in the war. Among the Arabs, double the numbers, between 10,000 and 12,000 died. For the Palestinian Arabs, it was a catastrophe. Some 750,000 Palestinian became refugees, were forced to live in one of 66 camps and lost 80% of historic Palestine.

David Ben Gurion, the Jewish leader during the war of independence, explained that England belonged to the English and Judea to the Jews. He was saying, in effect, that in Israel, there was only room for Jews. Almost 90% of the immigrating Jews settled on already existing Arab urban villages; they did not establish new settlements.

Around 485 Palestinian villages and 15 towns were destroyed during the war and ethnic cleansing. Jerusalem was divided—east and west—with the old walled city, including the holy sites, falling under Jordanian rule to the east and west Jerusalem being held by the Jews. These are the events that Palestinians called "*Al-Nakba*", literally (the catastrophe).

I recognize that this telling contradicts aspects of the Israeli national narrative that the Arabs attacked, Israel won, the Arabs left, and the Jews got the land. The real truth lies in the personal stories of those who survive, not Israel's self-congratulatory national narratives.

Please remember, in this part of the world, our homes and land are particularly important to us. It is considered a blessing to eat off our land. The healthier the land is, the better produce it gives, thus the better our well-being will be. So, losing our land meant losing our souls.

The Refugees and Catastrophe

One of the Arab blunders in the war—still felt today—was that overzealous field officers directed Palestinian Arabs to evacuate during the war, promising that within a few weeks, the armies would capture all of Palestine and return these citizens to their homes and lands.

They promised that not only would those who fled get their old property back, but they would get to take any Jewish holdings they desired. This explains why when Arab radio broadcasts ordered the civilian population of Palestinians to leave, many left thinking they would return shortly. It also explains why almost half of the Palestinian population ran away: one group fled for fear of the Israelis while the others were forced out, believing the promises of the Arab armies.

Meanwhile, the Jews worked to expel as many Palestinians as possible. For the population that did not leave willingly, the Jews rounded them up, often laying siege to and bombarding villages and population centers, setting fire to homes, properties, goods, expulsion, demolition, and finally, planting mines among the rubble to prevent any of the expelled inhabitants from returning. The main goal was to destroy the rural and urban areas of Palestine. The Israeli forces often fired shells near the villages at night, prompting many inhabitants to flee for their lives.

The typical strategy to drive the Palestinians away during the 1948 war was to attack and besiege them from three sides, leaving the fourth open to allow the inhabitants a way to flee. Men and women were separated into two groups. The women with children were sent to one area depending on the village's location but only after being stripped of their valuables. In some cases, young men were shot and killed in groups of four to six after an earlier group had been ordered to dig mass graves for them.

Other able-bodied men were taken to labor camps. Their immediate task was to bury the dead in other villages, demolish Arab houses, remove the debris from already demolished houses, and carry salvaged items to Jewish homes. They did arduous and dangerous jobs and were fed a slice of bread per day. They were kept in cramped concentration labor camps. The prisoners remained in Israeli camps for two to five years.

Sources of the Divide—Historical Background

Israel systematically demolished two-thirds of the Palestinian villages within their new borders. This was not done in the heat of the battle but was done well after the residents had fled or were driven out. These demolitions made it so that the refugees could not return and so that their lands could then be turned over to the new Jewish population.

The Palestinian Arabs who were expelled and fled were scattered in three different areas.

1. The 20% of Palestinians that remained within Israel proper after 1948 became refugees, often forced to relocate from their home villages and towns to other areas where they continued to live in the newly established State of Israel. Today, people call these Palestinians as Arab-Israelis. They are both Muslims and Christians, and they were relocated inside the land of what is now called Israel.

2. Many more of the Palestinian refugees went to East Jerusalem, the West Bank (Judea & Samaria), and the Gaza Strip. They were placed in 22 refugee camps that were initially made of tents. That became the Palestinians of the West Bank and the Gaza strip today.

3. The rest of the refugees fled to the neighboring Arab countries around the borders of the Land. Many went to Jordan, Syria, Lebanon, and even as far as Iraq and Egypt, forming the rest of the 44 refugee camps outside the land. These Arab nations, however, struggled to assimilate the refugees into their countries, and many remained dispossessed.

The impact of the catastrophe was traumatic for all the Palestinians, regardless of religion. Within the boundaries of the new State of Israel, many Arabs fled their homes to the neighboring countries, never to return.

Of the approximately 750,000 Palestinian Arabs who lost their precious land and ancestral homes, almost 50,000 were Christians. It is crucial to understand how the Palestinians, in general, and the Christians, in particular, were impacted. Wealthy members of the urban middle classes, who were lucky and had the resources, could escape in advance.

The elite of the Christian Palestinian society—including newspaper editors, doctors, dentists, architects, lawyers, businesspeople, and some politicians—lost all of their wealth to the invading Jews and had to start with nothing wherever they ended up. The Christian Palestinian middle class was almost completely erased. Many others were expelled during the war or were otherwise exiled, killed, or arrested. In other words, Palestinian Christians found themselves in all three of the above situations.

The war was particularly catastrophic for Jerusalem's indigenous Christian population. Most had lived in the western part of the city, having their summer houses outside the old city. All that territory fell to Israel. The Christians first fled to the eastern part of Jerusalem, losing everything they had. This devastated many, causing sickness and then death. They were forced to give up all their assets, and as educated members of the middle class, they had no choice but to accept the new conditions.

What is to be done of those who became refugees in 1948? In the aftermath of the war, Israel adopted a strict policy of preventing refugees from returning to their homes in the new state of Israel. Nearly a third of those refugees remained in the refugee camps; this remains true even until today.

Sources of the Divide—Historical Background

International law states clearly that refugees have the right to return to their homes and to receive compensation. So, there is a solution, but for some reason, it is not being implemented. Many Palestinian refugees still have the keys to their homes. The key has become a powerful emblem for Palestinian refugees, symbolizing their right to return.

These refugees continue to struggle. They have had little acceptance and have no future prospects. Whereas the Israeli population simply continued to enlarge. After the war, immigration became easier for the Jews. If you were Jewish, you had a right to return, even if you have never been to or seen the land before. Israel became the only country in the world that allowed you to emigrate based solely on religion. Whereas the Palestinian refugees who have been living in the land for generations have not been allowed to return.

After one year of fighting, a cease-fire agreement was reached. The agreement with the Jordanians, conducted in secret, stopped the war. The Armistice Lines of 1949 then became the boundary between Israel and the West Bank. The ink used to draw the boundary was green, giving the boundary its name, the Green Line. The line was recognized as Israel's border by the international community.

The West Bank was the territory on the west side of the Jordan River and allied with Jordan. The West Bank became a Jordanian territory west of the Jordan River, and the Palestinian people there were given Jordanian citizenship. Jerusalem was divided in half, east and west. The Jordanians took over rulership of the East half, especially the Old City. Palestinians living there were given Jordanian citizenship as well.

Gaza was given to Egypt as part of the deal. In return, the Jordanian king agreed not to prevent the establishment of the Jewish state, while the Jews would not prevent him from making the West Bank part of Jordan or of Gaza coming under the trusteeship of Egypt. Agreements were signed with Transjordan, Egypt, Lebanon, and Syria. Iraq refused to sign any agreement. That's how the Israeli border was drawn in green. And let's not forget that Israel gained control of 80% of historical Palestine.

Between the Two Wars

After the war, the Zionist movement convinced Arab Jews living in the other Arab countries to come to Israel. They were Jews, yes, but their home was the place in which they were born. They had few options, which is true, so they felt the need to go to their Promised Land where they believed it would be safer for them. These Jews from various Arab countries were more culturally social and accepted by the Palestinian community than the European Jews who often lived segregated lives, living in their own world. Among these Arab Jews, approximately 750,000 emigrated to Israel.

Because the Jews wanted more territory, from Dan to Beersheba, they also wanted most of the Sinai Peninsula, all of Transjordan, the whole northern portion of what is today Lebanon, and all of southwestern Syria, almost to the edge of Damascus. This represented the area of greater Israel.

To emphasize once again, the Israeli population doubled after the war. It was important that the Jewish numbers increased drastically after the war. These immigrants began settling high priority areas as well as in the Negev and Galilee to cement their hold on the region and build their fledgling state. Toward this end, Israel adopted the Absentee Property Law in 1950. This law said that anyone who was a Palestinian citizen in 1947 but had left his place of residence and had not returned was considered to have given up their rights to their property! This legalized Jewish possession of the property seized in 1948.

Even though the world recognized the State of Israel, the Zionists knew that what really mattered were facts on the ground. As Israel got stronger and more successful, Zionist support grew gradually stronger. At the height of the war and several years thereafter, the new state confronted a series of difficulties. The immense challenge of absorbing hundreds of thousands of Jewish immigrants into a country that had just emerged from a brutal war, lacked natural resources, and had an undeveloped economy, became its most significant challenge.

THE SIX DAYS WAR, 1967

In 1967, twenty years after the state of Israel was established, the bells of war rang once again. That year, President Jamal 'Abed El-Nasser of Egypt closed the Gulf of Aqaba to shipping, and Jordan entered a defense pact with Egypt a week before the war began. To preempt any Arab attack from the new alliance, Israel struck Egypt and destroyed most of the Egyptian air force while it was still on the ground at air bases. This sparked the war. Israel fought alone against Jordan, Syria, and Egypt.

In less than a week, Israel seized and occupied the Gaza Strip and the Sinai Peninsula from Egypt. They captured the West Bank (including East Jerusalem) from Jordan, and the Golan Heights were taken from Syria. The war was fought between June fifth and tenth, a mere six days. That's how it received its name, 'The Six Day War.' In the aftermath, Israel had crippled Egyptian, Syrian, and Jordanian militaries, killing over 20,000 troops while losing fewer than 1,000 of its own.

Once again, the displacement of Palestinian civilian populations due to the six days war would have long-term consequences. Between 280,000 and 325,000 Palestinians fled or were expelled from the West

Bank and Gaza, becoming refugees for the second time! They fled mainly to Jordan and some to Egypt as in the case of my family that left from Jaffa to Egypt. Over 100,000 fled from the Golan Heights farther north to Syria, which opened the door for Israel to demolish hundreds of Palestinian villages. At the same time, the rest of the Jewish minority communities fled or were expelled from Arab countries, and most came to Israel.

Despite all, the Palestinians who fled as refugees for the seconded time, have never stopped hoping to return to their land and homes. As a result of the 1967 war, the gap separating Arabs and Jews widened further, and the suffering of the Palestinian people increased. That said, the war allowed Israel to take what it had originally wanted in 1948 but lacked the resources or political expediency back then. The result cannot be denied: now Israel had reclaimed the rest 20% of the land of their promise.

From a Zionist perspective, this was unbelievable. Palestine was erased from the map. Getting rid of Palestinians and de-Arabizing the country was imperative for the Israel state. The population went from a Jewish minority to a Jewish majority in less than a hundred years.

Since 1967, many events have shaped the conflict between Palestinians and Israelis. The most important ones include the development of the Palestinian Liberation Organization (PLO), the Yom Kippur War (1973), the First Palestinian Intifada (1987-1993), the Oslo Accords (1993-1999), the Second Intifada (2000-2004), the construction of the Separation Barrier (2002-2006), Hamas' Rule in Gaza and Israeli Blockade (2006-present).

I could easily write a chapter on each, but that would make this book much too long. For now, I will summarize by simply stating that the 1948 war of Israel's establishment and the Six-Day war of 1967, in which Israel occupied additional Palestinian territories, like the Golan

Sources of the Divide—Historical Background

Heights, The West Bank and Gaza Strip as well as the Sinai Peninsula, were these two wars were the two primary sources of the divide that we see today between Jews and Palestinians.

The Present Impasse: Five Key Issues

Before I move to the next part of the book, I would like to share five keys to the conflict. If you can remember these, they will keep you from getting lost in all the details of the history. These five issues must be resolved for there to be lasting peace: The refugees, settlements, Jerusalem, water, and borders.

Refugees: Today, more than seven million Palestinians live outside Palestine. Many are refugees and still live in refugee camps in Lebanon, Jordan, and Syria. There are 44 camps in these countries, and in Palestine, there are an additional 22. But not all Palestinian refugees still live in camps. They live in many countries worldwide and maintain their refugee status. The question of their right of return is at the heart of the Israel-Palestine conflict. And, at a minimum, they need to be compensated for the loss of their property.

Settlements: Israel has built many settlements inside Palestinian territory in the West Bank and East Jerusalem. Born of an ideology of conquest, the Israeli settlements are one of the most challenging points of the peace negotiations because the expansion of the settlements in the West Bank and East Jerusalem has continued without pause since 1967. These mostly armed, settlers have been allotted the best of the arable land in the areas they occupy. Settlements in the old city of Hebron are a good example. Among approximately 150,000 Palestinians, about 500 settlers live in the heart of Hebron with heavy military protection.

Jerusalem: Israelis and Palestinians both claim Jerusalem as their capital. Israel considers all of Jerusalem its eternal capital, including East Jerusalem. But for Palestinians, East Jerusalem is occupied territory and Israel's annexation of it has never been recognized by international law. Palestinians claim East Jerusalem as the capital of the future Palestinian state, which is why all the embassies of the world are situated in Tel Aviv. When the United States recently moved its embassy to Jerusalem, they were saying, in effect, that Jerusalem is for Jews only and no longer for Palestinians. Israel is doing all it can to make the city more Jewish, making it harder for the Palestinians to realize their dream of getting it back.

Water: The division and use of water and other natural resources. Many aquafers are in the mountains of the West Bank, which means that Palestinians should control them. But Israel does not permit that. Israel controls them—and inequitably, giving abundant provision to Jewish areas while limiting Palestinian areas severely. This is a profound injustice. Israel uses seven times more water than the Palestinians and prevents Palestinians from using more. Palestinians in the West Bank don't even receive fresh water every day. To get by, many have dug cisterns that fill with rain. They use the water for agriculture or cleaning. On the other side, Israelis have an abundant, direct, and strong water flow daily. They don't store water because it is almost never cut off.

. . .

Sources of the Divide—Historical Background

Borders: A must address are the issues of borders, security, and sovereignty—who has complete control of which territories. The promise of peace where Israelis and Palestinians can live side-by-side in separate countries would require extensive bypass roads, bridges, tunnels, and so forth. As things stand, Palestinian villages in Israel would need to be disconnected from Israel, while Jewish settlements in Palestine would need to be connected to Israel. From the standpoint of infrastructure, implementing such a solution would be very complicated and confusing, not to mention devastating for the natural environment and the historical beauty of the land. Both Israelis and Palestinians want security and sovereignty. But how can you draw the map?

If you remember these five—refugees, settlements, Jerusalem, water, and borders— you are on your way to understanding how the bridge has come to be hidden. Even though history and politics have hidden the presence of Christians, they remain scattered throughout the land, obeying the teachings of Jesus, and faithfully loving God and their neighbors.

Between 1948 and 1967, the Christian population of Jerusalem dropped from 35% of the total population to 15% (as of this writing in 2022, we the Christians are now only 1% of the population of Jerusalem).

Each Christian is an essential part of the bridge, no matter where God has placed us. In Part 2, I explain the history and biblical stories associated with different places and geographic areas. I also share about all the Christians in these areas, their challenges and how they are living like Christ faithfully.

Chapter 2

We, the Christians of the land, are closely connected to Jesus through culture, language, history, and geography. Understanding him in this context teaches us how to be this bridge. He is our foundation—our inspiration and vision. But the vision and bridge have been hidden from others through history and politics. Even though Christians are scattered throughout the land, I will share how they keep living faithfully.

Part Two

The Hidden Bridge and its Parts

Chapter 3. Who are the Holyland Christians?

Chapter 4. Christians in Israel Proper

Chapter 5. Christians of the West Bank and Gaza Strip

Chapter 6. Christians from Jerusalem

Chapter 7. Christian Believers from a Muslim Background

Chapter 8. Christian Believers from a Jewish Background

PART TWO

*The Heart of the Via Dolorosa in the Old City Jerusalem:
Notice the Menorah in the middle the most ancient Jewish symbol,
the cross to the right of the flag, is the Christian sign of faith, and the
Minaret to the left the Muslim mark of prayer.*

Chapter 3

Who are the Holyland Christians?

(The Quest for Identity)

Christians in the Holyland are the hidden bridge, and that bridge consists of multiple parts. Each part works together and contributes to the whole. The spirit of Christ brings them together and connects them as one. At the same time, each piece has its unique contributions and challenges, social location and geography, purpose and role. In the following chapters, I look at each part of the bridge in turn.

I introduce Palestinian Christians in this chapter. I offer a brief overview of them as a community, looking at their origins, social contributions, and challenges. This chapter is a springboard for the following three chapters, where I discuss more details and specifics about them as a community based on their geographic region.

The Origins of Palestinian Christians

The term Palestine for the first time occurs in the work of the Greek historian Herodotus, who lived in the middle of the fifth century BC.

CHAPTER 3

Later, in the second century AD, the Romans adopted this term as the administrative name for the region. Palestine, as a stand-alone term, came into widespread use after that time. We know that it was printed on coins. It has been found on ancient inscriptions and was even written in the rabbinic texts.

Moreover, from the height of Britain imperial reign until the end of their Mandate, the British officially used the term Palestinian to describe all communities living in the Holyland, regardless of whether they were describing Jews, Christians, or Muslims. In other words, the name Palestinian was applied to all people living in this area up until the creation of Israel in 1948.

If calling Arab Christians "Palestinian" is still a challenge for you after reading the previous chapter, please remember that Palestine is simply one of the historical names for the land surrounded by Lebanon, Syria, Jordan, and Egypt. Today, most of this land is now Israel.

So, the term Palestinian is commonly applied to the Arabs and their descendants who live—or once lived—in the area historically known as Palestine. Some have remained in the land, but many fled in 1948 and 1967, as we discussed previously. Palestinians are the mixed descendants of three main groups:

1. The Canaanites, Hittites, and Amorites, all of whom were of the same race.
2. The Philistines, who were the people of the sea.
3. The Bedouins of the desert, that is the Arabs from the Arabian Peninsula.

In other words, Palestinians are descendants of ancient Canaanites, Philistines, Bedouins, other Middle Easterners (Arameans), and even some Europeans who moved to and lived in Palestine since ancient times. One dimension contributing to their diverse origins is that Palestine was the corridor between Europe, Africa, and Asia. Many people came and went through the corridor, mixing over time. Most of these people were Arabized in the early Islamic period between the seventh and tenth centuries AD.

You might be amazed to learn that, today, there is more Jewish blood in the local Palestinian community than in the blood of many new Jewish immigrants from Europe and other places. This speaks to both the amount of mixing between peoples throughout the centuries and the complexity of Palestinians and Jewish ethnic categories.

Currently, there are almost 14 million Palestinians in the world. They have a strong sense of their Palestinian identity and believe it needs to be expressed in the form of a Palestinian state. Roughly half of them continue to live in the region of historic Palestine, an area encompassing Israel proper (one and a half million), the West Bank (three and a half million), and the Gaza Strip (two million) and about 350,000 in East Jerusalem. The remaining seven million Palestinians comprise what is known as the Palestinian diaspora, living in neighboring Jordan, Syria, Lebanon, Saudi Arabia, and other western countries.

Interestingly, there are almost seven million Jews in Israel and another seven million in the USA and other countries. This adds up to roughly 14 million, nearly the same number as the Palestinians. So, there are seven million Palestinians and seven million Jews in the Holyland and seven million Palestinians and seven million Jews worldwide.

And of the seven million Palestinians living in the diaspora, roughly 700,000 are Christian. While this may seem like a large number, it means that less than one percent of the Palestinian population is today Christian. These Palestinian Christians in the diaspora reside in many different places, in countries such as Argentina, Australia, Brazil, Canada, Chile, Colombia, Cuba, the Dominican Republic, Mexico, the United States, and Venezuela.

There are also many in Europe, especially in the United Kingdom, France, and Spain, and to a lesser extent, in Ireland, Germany, Italy, Greece, and the Netherlands. The Palestinian Christians are known for having multiple international experiences and connections to different countries, yet the place they have the most difficulty relating to is their home in historic Palestine.

My two aunts, for example, who were both born here in the land, now live in the United States. They can come back to visit, but Israel will never permit them to live here. Since I already discussed the issue of Palestinian refugees and the barriers Israel has created for Palestinians returning to their land, I will not repeat that information here. I will only briefly mention that I know of an Arab Christian family who wanted to convert to Judaism in order to return, but they were turned back at the airport. That's how much Palestinians long to return, yet they are prevented.

Within the land, three main groups of Palestinian Christians were created by the establishment of the state of Israel and subsequent political developments:

First, the Palestinian Christians who remain in Israel. They are often called Arab Israelis. They live in cities such as Haifa and Nazareth, and many other Galilean villages. **Second, there are the Christians of the West Bank and the Gaza Strip.** These Christians are concentrated in cities such as Ramallah and Bethlehem and scattered in various villages throughout the West Bank. **And third, the Palestinian Christians of East Jerusalem** of whom I am part of and where I was born and still live there until today.

Who are the Holyland Christians?

As of 2022, Palestinian Christians make up less than two percent of the population of Israel and less than one percent of the Palestinian population in the West Bank and Gaza. About 180,000 Christian citizens of Israel, about 50,000 Christians in the West Bank, around 800 Christians living in the whole Gaza Strip, and less than 10,000 Christians in East Jerusalem (out of the one million citizens of today's Jerusalem). Although our numbers are small, Palestinian Christians play important roles in the Holyland.

How do we Contribute to the society?

Palestinian Christians are characterized by their high education levels, political involvement, and ability to represent their people's cause to the outside world. Over the years, Palestinian Christians have built numerous institutions that serve both the Christian but mainly the Muslim communities. They lead schools, hospitals, vocational training colleges, and libraries. These contributions help integrate them into society and create goodwill with our neighbors of the other religious communities, that is Jews and Muslims.

Education is vital for Palestinian Christians. Many become doctors, chemists, and professionals in every field. Almost all of the Palestinian Christians of the land speak at least three languages fluently. Women are no longer expected to stay at home either but are often highly qualified. Most have jobs outside the home. Palestinian Christians are the most educated people among all the Arab nations.

The Christians in the land predominantly attend private Christian schools. And, in a way, we have no choice. Even though private Christian schools are more expensive than public government schools, we still send our children to private Christian schools because it would be extremely hard for our children in government schools, as a minority between Jews or Muslims where the curriculum is oriented toward other faith traditions.

That said, when I call a private school or university 'Christian,' I mean that it was founded by Christians but may not be currently led by them. This does not mean the student population is Christian. Bethlehem university, for example, one of the principal universities in Palestine, is a Christian institution but only about ten percent of the teachers and students are Christian. The rest are Muslim. Although we are a minority, the Christians of the land are responsible for educating almost 25% of the Arab Palestinian population in the Arab-Israel cities and in the West Bank and Gaza strip as well as in East Jerusalem.

Many Christian hospitals serve in the major Arab cities, like the English Hospital in Nazareth. There are also a few orphanages that serve in the West Bank and other Muslim communities. Many companies were founded by Christians originally, like the International Arab Bank and the International Deloitte accounting company. Although they are mainly in local Muslim hands now, they were once started by Christians.

What are some of our Challenges?

Despite these outstanding contributions, Palestinian Christians face numerous challenges within their own society. One challenge is economic. During the two *"Intifadas"* meaning uprisings, the First intifada (1987- 1993); and the second Intifada (2000- 2004), many Christian-owned businesses closed. People sold their property, emigrated away, and many others lost employment.

Another challenge is social. There is an apparent campaign by most Jews in Israel and Muslims in the West Bank to take over the neighborhoods and work. In Israel, a national policy gives preference to potential employees who have served in the Israeli army. This means Palestinians Christians have fewer opportunities for employment since they do not serve in the Jewish armed forces. Something similar happens in the West Bank where Muslims get priority.

This fact limits Palestinian Christians substantially. That said, even the Christians who do find work face challenges because not only do they feel alone due to the lack of Christian colleagues, but others do not want them around because of their Christian integrity.

Even in Christian schools, kids can be bullied just because they are Christians. This often creates an identity crisis in our children. They struggle with who they are, and with whom to identify. Take my children for example. My kids are affected by other kids in their school telling them they must hate the Jews. They come home and repeat these things to me. Even though I tell them that we Christians should love everybody and not hate even those who have harmed us, they still feel pressure to be patriotic and fight the Jews.

Another challenge is the psychological pressure. Should our kids and the youth leaders leave, or should they stay in a dangerous environment? Christians face massive spiritual warfare in the land. Christ overcame the devil on the cross and rose again. The spirit of Islam and Judaism both reject Jesus. In fact, the religious Jews see us as even more dangerous than they do the Muslims. The spirit of Judaism rejects Jesus as Lord and Savior, whereas in the eyes of Muslims, we are infidels.

There is no Palestinian Christian in the land who has not been harmed by Jewish pride and arrogance or by Muslim hate and aggression. The Jews see themselves as superior and chosen by God, better than any other nation. Meanwhile, Muslims are becoming more violent because they are desperate to defend themselves, as we the

Palestinian Christian Arabs can understand well, both of their religions.

Christians are, thus, crushed between the weight of two different extremisms and face the challenge of continuing witness to the presence of a loving God in this land and the bearers of His message to both the Jewish and Muslim majorities.

Christians also experience direct persecution. This has happened throughout history but has intensified during the Arab Spring. In Israel proper and East Jerusalem, we can call this persecution more like discrimination, where we have faced challenges in areas like housing and employment. But in the West Bank and the Gaza Strip, this discrimination can sometimes become violent persecution.

Given these challenges, it should not surprise you that many Palestinian Christians have chosen to emigrate elsewhere, leaving Palestine. The socio-economic and political situation continues to be the main reason for this departure. The collapse of peace is forcing more and more Christians to emigrate because they want to find better futures for their children.

This means the Palestinian Christian presence is dwindling in the Holyland. Many young leaders are simply leaving. And, frankly, it is hard to blame them. There is no longer a single village or city in the West Bank or Israel that is solely Christian. The life of a minority that wishes to preserve its identity is generally challenging.

The majority of Palestinian Christians now live in the diaspora. If the trend of outward immigration continues, the Holyland will turn into a museum of Christian history, visited only by Christian pilgrims and tourists. In other words, one of our main challenges is simply staying. We must rise above the political pressure, neither taking sides in

Jewish- Muslim problems nor abandoning our calling as the hidden bridge.

We are living among two nations where religion is part of their nationality. But Christians generally should not think that way. Instead, we have the critical task of continuing to be witnesses of the love of God and the bearers of His message in the land.

Keeping The Hidden Bridge Hanging Firm

One question I am often asked is this: Why do you stay? Would it not be easier to move somewhere else since there are so many troubles between Jews and Muslims? My simple answer is this—God, in his divine wisdom, chose for me to be born here. I cannot run away from that. I must also practice Jesus' words in order to live by them. If I lose my life for the Gospel's sake, I shall find it.

Indeed, Christians who stay in the Middle East sacrifice a lot. But we find our life in Christ by doing the will of God. We should shine in the midst of the darkness, aiming to obey and take responsibility. We must keep our faith strong and move forward to fulfill God's dream. In Christ, it is all worth it. Palestinian Christians must be strong and different. We should strive to excel in education and business, maintaining a lifestyle that allows us to function in the greater community of Jews and Muslims.

We, Christians, need to face our fears as Jesus met His. Jesus did not run from the cross in the Garden of Gethsemane. He could have just walked up the Mount of Olives on the road to Jericho and gotten lost in the desert. But He didn't.

We need to be as close to God as Jesus was to His Father so we can face our fears. Christians need to be witnesses of God's love. We must be a barrier against hatred, fear, unforgiveness, ignorance, and war.

I also believe that moving the Christian society out of Israel proper, the West Bank- Gaza, and East Jerusalem, will cause us to lose the credibility of our witness reaching out with the Gospel to our own people, both Jews and Muslims. Loving your own people is essential. It is not a sin to identify with them, even if others have negative ideas about them. We Christians have a responsibility to share with our own people.

We are called to let our light shine, to witness and serve our community. It was God's plan for us to be born in this nation. We grew up knowing the language, culture, and customs of all the people of the land, so we know well. We have gained the experience of how to identify with both the Jews and the Muslims of the land.

In fact, when conflicts happen in middle eastern culture, you need a third party to mediate. God has put Palestinian Christians in the best position to help. We understand the injustices and problems, and we take nonviolent steps to help both sides. We know both Jews and Muslims—their cultures and languages—and we follow the teachings of Jesus.

If peace is going to happen, it will be because the people in the land want it. We need to build bridges to understand and accept one another. God has placed Christians here to be the bridge between the two people.

There is no Christianity without a cross, for without the crucifixion, there is no resurrection. On the cross, we see the love of God. To demonstrate our love to others, we must carry our cross, too. God's love includes all people. In Jesus Christ, we have hope. We, the Christians of this land, pray for all the people of the land, whether Jews or Muslims, despite our daily challenges.

This is the real love that requires sacrifice and paying the price so that the only hope for all the people of the land is this love that God has planted in our hearts. Our faith is that the Lord will give them enlightenment so that they will accept Christ. There is much power in prayer. This is how God will bring them to salvation.

We ask that God would use us in His work and that He would put compassion in our hearts to stand for our people. The seeds have been planted, and now is the time that they should start to sprout. But for this to happen, the seeds need self-denial so the roots can grow and bring fruit. Then, everyone can reap and enjoy the taste of God's love for all His creation.

My grandfather, whom I mentioned at the beginning of the book, the one who took us on his strolls, he was a farmer. He told me to stay firm like an olive tree, unshaken by the wind. The olive tree is an evergreen, a symbol of continuous hope and life. The tree produces olives, and, in ancient times, the oil made from those olives was used to light people's homes. We Christians are like the oil Jesus will use to bring light into the darkness.

Yes, Christians are a small minority, but they are the bridge that is hidden throughout the country. I have been all over Israel and Palestine, trying to encourage Christians. I've visited established church congregations and small groups that meet in homes. I've visited Muslim background believers and Messianic Jews. And I'm encouraged that there are believers in almost every village and city from the north to the south of this country. In the following chapters, I share some of what I have learned from each of them. I share details about their hopes and challenges and their links to Jesus through the Bible and geography.

Chapter 3

The Oldest Tree at the Garden of Gethsemane

Chapter 4

Christians in Israel Proper
(The Arab-Israelis)

This chapter is about the Arab-Israeli Christians. Since most Arab-Israeli Christians live in the Galilee area, in the northern part of the Holyland, especially in the Nazareth area. I begin the chapter with a discussion of the background and history of the city, followed by a discussion of Jesus' childhood in the city. I then talk about the present situation of Arab-Israeli Christians in Israel and offer a few reflections on the significance of this part of Jesus's life to me.

Background and History of Nazareth

Why were people in the first century ready for the Messiah to come? This question can only be answered by understanding the historical background and formation of the village of Nazareth.

One of the earliest Jewish revolts was the Maccabean rebellion against the Greeks. The uprising took place against the Seleucids around the second century BC and produced the Hasmonean dynasty that ruled for one hundred years. That means the Maccabees are the founding fathers of the Hasmonean dynasty of Jewish rulers and priests. The Hasmoneans are the descendants of Mattathias the Maccabean and his sons.

This was the first Jewish reign of the land since King David. However, one remarkable feature of the Hasmonean dynasty is that its leaders were kings and priests simultaneously. They controlled both the political and religious landscape. Though the Maccabeans started out piously enough, in the end, they became more corrupt than the Greeks. This corruption, in turn, led to the people becoming fed up with their kings. They wanted God to return and save them from the oppression of their leaders.

Before this, Galilee had been controlled by Gentiles for the previous six or seven hundred years. Jewish towns in Galilee were essentially wiped off the map by the Assyrian military campaigns from (740- 720) BC, particularly the campaign of Tiglath-Pileser III. The towns lay in ruins until slightly before 100 BC.

Then, in 103 BC, during the reign of one of the main Hasmonean kings, Alexander Jannaeus, the Hasmoneans attempted to Judaize the Galilee and bring the Jewish presence back into the region. In this effort, Alexander also forced the people in the south, the Idumeans, to become Jews. One prominent example of an Idumean who was forced to convert to Judaism was Antipater. He was the grandfather of Herod the Great. Does that name sound familiar?

Some of the towns Alexander Jannaeus rebuilt in the Galilee region were Nazareth, Nain, Capernaum, Bethsaida, Chorazin, and Magdalah. Most of the people who resettled them were Jews from Judea. This explains how and why both Mary, the mother of Jesus, and Joseph were residents of Nazareth who traced their ancestry to Bethlehem in Judea.

In fact, most (if not all) Jews in the Galilean villages of Jesus' day could trace their ancestry to Judea. And since they did not like paying taxes, they developed the habit of leaving the area temporarily whenever the Romans called for a census, since they used censuses to determine taxes. Not to be outsmarted, the Romans issued a decree that every Roman subject had to return to their place of origin to be counted for the census. For the people of Nazareth, that would be about a five-day journey on foot. They could be arrested if they were not there at the time of the census.

Since Nazareth had only been occupied for 130 years at the time of Jesus' birth, most sources say there would have only been two-to-three hundred people living in the city. That would have been about 25 extended Jewish families. That's it. There were barely enough people for a synagogue. Needless to say, Nazareth was not that big or important. It didn't even have walls.

It may sound funny, but the most important thing to remember about Nazareth is that Nazareth was not important. By contrast, the city of Cana, not too far from Nazareth, had a population of nearly 10,000 people at the time. This fact partly explains why Nathanael, when Jesus called him to be his disciple, said, "Nazareth! Can anything good come from there?" Nathanael was from Cana. He couldn't believe something great would come from such a small, insignificant place. Nazareth was the city people made fun of in Galilee.

Worse, a teenage Jewish girl from Nazareth was even less significant. At that time, girls did not go to school. For the New Testament to include a story about an angel of God appearing to Mary, who was probably around 15 years old, would have been astounding. Even laughable.

Chapter 4

The Roman governor, Pontius Pilate, likely found humor in the sign he had nailed to Jesus' cross: "Jesus of Nazareth, the King of the Jews." He was clearly mocking Jesus. Likewise, Jesus never studied in the scribal schools where the famous Rabbis were training. Jesus came from a small, out-of-the-way town. In fact, Nazareth was so small that it was never mentioned in the Old Testament, even though it had existed from ancient times.

Geographically, Nazareth is situated in a beautiful valley guarded by the Nazareth Mountains in Lower Galilee. One of the main interpretations of the Hebrew word "Nazareth" is 'to guard,' likely hinting that the town was guarded by the surrounding mountains. The city has also been called 'the Flower of Galilee' since, from afar, the seven mountains that surround it look like a flower.

In Hebrew, the three-letter root for the word Nazareth is *N-Z-R* or "*Netzer*", and it connotes the idea of an offshoot or branch. People may have believed that a good name for their village was Nazareth since the Assyrians had cut off Nazareth and left a stump.

Christians in Israel today are called "*Notsrim*". This is a Hebrew word coming from the same root. A shepherd uses a "*Netzer*" to guard his sheep. Jesus was also called a Nazarene. After an olive tree is cut down, it sends up offshoots from around the root called "*Netzarim*". Interestingly, (Isaiah 11:1) says, "a *Netzer* (shoot) will come up from the stump of Jesse."

It was from Nazareth that the birth of Christ was announced. It was where His parents, Joseph and the Virgin Mary, had their home and where He was raised. What better name could there be for their village than the offshoot of Jesse? It's clear that God chose a specific people, at a specific time, in a specific place, to forward His Kingdom. God used the most unlikely of people from the most unlikely of places to do one of the most extraordinary things he has ever done in history.

The Basilica of the Annunciation Main Façade
The Word Became Flesh and Dwelt Among Us

Chapter 4

The Announcement and Jesus' Childhood

In (Isaiah 7:14), we read the prophecy, "Therefore the Lord Himself will give you a sign: Behold, the virgin shall conceive and bear a Son, and shall call His name Immanuel". And then we find its fulfillment in the gospel of Luke when the Angel of the Lord came to the virgin Mary and announces that she will have a child, (Luke 1:26-38).

The New Testament does not mention exactly where Mary was when the angel Gabriel appeared to her. Was she at home or out at a well getting water? In the Jewish rabbinic tradition, a Jewish girl in a small village rarely went beyond her house or the well without other girls or her man. Here was Mary, this ordinary young girl, and God chose her. God chose her because she was willing to obey. God knew she would be obedient despite the pain it would cause her, having people mock and doubt her pregnancy.

Even Joseph pondered leaving her. He was shocked and doubtful about the validity of her immaculate conception story until God told him to take care of Mary and the baby. Joseph was no dreamer. He was a hardworking man. But one night, after he finally fell asleep, God revealed His plan to him through a dream and erased all his suspicions.

Imagine what this situation would have been like for everyone else, everyone except Joseph and Mary. In the first century, the engagement period for a young couple was typically a test to ensure they were compatible. But shortly after her engagement, Mary finds herself pregnant without having ever slept with a man. She starts claiming that the child in her womb is from the Holy Spirit. Of course, everyone would suspect adultery. And Jewish law said that the punishment for that was stoning or being cast out. It would have been Joseph's job to inform the community. If she were not stoned to death, she would have to stay alone for the rest of her life without a husband. Her family would disown her. Nobody would accept her. She would be forced to beg for a living and perhaps become a harlot to scrape by. What a mess!

Mary nevertheless accepted the announcement. She willingly paid the price, and her obedience brought God's salvation and blessings to the entire world. The hard decisions shape our lives and bring us blessings, not the easy, normal ones. God can do the impossible. He can use every day and ordinary people to make an uncommon and extraordinary difference. What a great way he shows his love to us! Whatever God's will be for your life, you should accept it because He is the God of the impossible. True faith will always be manifested in obedience.

Another aspect of this story I enjoy pondering is that Luke, the gospel writer, was a doctor. He would have known precisely how women conceived and gave birth. Tradition tells us that Luke personally spoke with Mary before writing his gospel's first two chapters. I sometimes wonder if he had trouble believing her as she recounted the story to him. For someone with medical training, it is simply inconceivable that a virgin would birth a child. Yet through her testimony, Luke came to believe that God, the Creator, placed a child in her virgin womb. And he chose to pass that story to us, in extraordinary, divine detail.

Now, fast forward past Jesus' birth in Bethlehem (we'll get into that in the next chapter) and imagine Jesus, the kid back in Nazareth, going to play with other kids on His way to get water from the well with His mother. Would Mary have been mocked then? Sadly, I have no answer to this question, but the other kids of Nazareth would have mocked Jesus stealing his kippa!

Chapter 4

Also, it is important to remember about Nazareth is that Jesus lived there most of His life, from childhood until he started his ministry. Life expectancy in the first century only went to someone's 40's. Since Jesus began his ministry at about age 30, that meant he lived almost three-fourths of his life in the city of Nazareth.

A young child from a humble family in a small, insignificant Galilean village would become the instrument by which the entire world would date their calendars. Two thousand years ago, Jesus was a small boy, perhaps about the age of four, playing in the streets of Nazareth. Joseph was a carpenter and builder, and as Jesus grew, He followed in his father's trade as was the custom of that time.

Wait—was Joseph really a carpenter? I said that casually in the last sentence, but is it true? Not by today's standards or meaning. The original Greek word for Joseph's trade is *"tecton"*. The word means more 'to form or make.' Carpenter is an unfortunate translation because if Joseph worked as a carpenter only, he would not be able to make a living and provide for his family.

The word *"tecton"* indicates the profession of one who comes and oversees a construction site, calculates how much stone and wood is needed, cuts the stone and wood, and plans the building. Today, Joseph would be considered a contractor who does everything and takes responsibility for the finished project. So, a *"tecton"* is a pious, deeply educated man who builds and creates.

As a builder in a land full of stones in an era before specialization, it's quite possible that Joseph quarried stones and built walls. Almost everything was made of stone then, and nearly all Joseph's jobs would have been stonemason work. The geology of Nazareth indicates a lot of chalk in the hills. Because chalk is easy to work with, people carved out basements, silos, cisterns, cellars, and storerooms. As a builder of homes, Joseph would have worked with wood, too. The rough trunks of small trees would have become roof beams.

Jesus followed His earthly father's vocation and became a *tecton*. And if you pay attention, you will notice that Jesus' sermons used illustrations from stonemasonry more than carpentry. Scholars believe one of the main reasons the holy family moved to Nazareth in the first place was because Joseph could secure work in Sepphoris, the city near Nazareth that would become the capital of the Galilee.

Sepphoris was home to some 30,000 people at the time. Indeed, Jesus would have helped His father in Sepphoris since it was only a two-hour walk from Nazareth. Through this experience and others, Jesus was likely exposed to Greek and Roman cultures and languages. He had a job and likely began work at age 13 and continued until he started his ministry.

We also know that Jesus grew up in a righteous family. He grew up being taught the scriptures, as his biblical knowledge demonstrates throughout the gospels. He spoke on His own authority and not on the authority of His teachers. His humble beginning in Nazareth was no mistake.

It takes time to prepare to build the Kingdom of God. God uses everything in our lives, all the natural experiences and the small things we pass through, to prepare us for the spiritual work He has called us to. No matter how little we own or how few our talents might be, once we put them in the hands of God, He will be able to use them in a mighty way. Jesus' three years of ministry were shaped by the 30 years he spent growing up in Nazareth.

Chapter 4

Nazareth First Century Map

Christians in Israel Proper

The Arab-Israeli Christians of Nazareth and Surrounding Villages

The Arab citizens of Israel mostly live in Arab majority towns and cities. Generally speaking, supporters of Israel tend to use Arab Israeli to refer to this population without mentioning Palestine. While supporters of Palestinians tend to use the term, the Palestinians of 1948 without referencing Israel. The term Arab Israelis is viewed as a construct of the Israel authorities.

Today, asking an Arab-Israeli Christian to identify themselves can be a little confusing. You won't get a straightforward answer—like French, British, or Italian. The answer is more complicated, and some explanation almost always follows their statement. They are Christians but also Arabs. They are Palestinian but also Israeli. Add to this the bureaucratic gymnastics they have had to perform to reunite with friends and family from the West Bank, Gaza, and East Jerusalem.

Without question, they are Palestinian Arabs, and they identify with their fellow Palestinians on many issues. But the picture gets fuzzy and contorted, especially when their daily immersion in the Hebrew language and Jewish culture begins to rub off on them. Some of them have even developed a level of identification with Jewish Israelis.

All these complications stem from their legal status in relation to other Palestinians and their growing integration within Jewish-Israeli society. Therefore, the majority of the Arab Israelis identify themselves as Arab or Palestinian by nationality and as Israeli by citizenship.

It took a long time for Arab-Israelis to gain enough power to claim citizenship in Israel. They pursued it to get more benefits for themselves in the Israeli society. Because of this citizenship, they are

CHAPTER 4

legally defined as Israelis rather than Palestinians. They have Israeli passports. They have the right to vote in Israel government elections. They have elected representatives in the Knesset (the Israeli Parliament). Arab-Israelis can even choose to serve in the Israeli police and army if they want.

Contrast this with Palestinians in the West Bank or Gaza, who are not allowed to enter Israel. They can serve in neither the Israeli police nor the army, and they have Palestinian passports. Likewise, Palestinians in East Jerusalem are considered residents of Israel but not citizens. They have Jordanian passports. They cannot serve in the Israeli army, but they can work in the Israeli police only.

Keeping all this straight can become a challenge quickly. But don't worry. I explain these issues regarding Palestinians in the West Bank, Gaza, and East Jerusalem more clearly in the following two chapters. The main point is that Arab-Israelis are more integrated into the Jewish-Israeli system than any other Arab Palestinians of East Jerusalem, The West Bank and the Gaza Strip.

To add, the Arab-Israelis attend different schools than Jewish kids within Israel, though they share the same Jewish curriculum. As generally they attend schools that are separated to some degree from those of Jewish though they have to go by the same program and examinations called the *"Bagrut"*. That curriculum emphasizes Hebrew and teaches Israeli history. So, for example, Arabs are taught the significance of Israel's Independence Day and celebrate it while, in contrast, they are taught virtually nothing about the *"Nakba"*, the Palestinian catastrophe of 1948 we discussed in Chapter 2.

And across the board, Arab-Israeli schools receive less funding from the state than their Jewish counterparts. Only when they reach university do Arab-Israelis and Jews interact on more equal footing. Their long-term presence in the Israeli school system explains why

Christians in Israel Proper

Arab-Israelis can speak Hebrew fluently, unlike their fellow Arabs in the West Bank, Gaza, and East Jerusalem, where public schools are in Arabic and private Christian schools are typically in different foreign languages as French, German, Spanish and less Hebrew.

Despite many of the rights they enjoy as citizens, Arab-Israeli citizens claim they are second-class citizens, pointing out discrimination on various levels. They point to a lack of government investment in Arab areas, unfair and continued expropriation of their land, and projects intended to Judaize areas with high Arab populations. Obtaining Jobs is also harder for Arab-Israelis than Jews since Jewish businesses often require military service before employment, inhibiting the possibility of Arab-Israeli employment for those who don't serve in the Israeli army, which is most.

The contemporary form of secular democracy in Israel appears to be the system most able to provide Arab-Israelis with the opportunity to flourish, contribute to civic life, and shape their destiny. Although the State of Israel has striven to embody such a system, the ambiguity of its simultaneous desire to be Jewish coupled with the radicalization of many of its Jewish citizens in response to the ongoing conflict with Arabs is making it increasingly difficult for such a goal to be realized. Arab-Israelis must often struggle to achieve equal treatment with their Jewish co-citizens.

This helps explain why those Arab-Israelis who have developed more identification with the Israeli state will, nevertheless, continue to feel like they are being kept at an arm's distance. The example that puts this tension in the most vivid terms is Israel's national anthem. The song is written from the perspective of a diaspora Jew yearning to emigrate to Zion. How could any Arab sing such a song —no matter how integrated they feel—when their friends and family, their Palestinian kin, were pushed out from their historical homeland—and kept away—to make room for these new Jewish immigrants?

Moreover, within the Israeli political sphere, the phrase demographic threat is used to describe the growth of Arab Israelis as constituting a threat to its maintenance of its status as a Jewish state with a Jewish demographic majority. As their increasing population, Muslims have the highest birth rate, this has become more a growing point of open political contention in recent years.

Now, focusing more specifically on Christians, of which the majority live in the northern parts of Israel, representing the majority of Christians in the whole of the land today. Among them, there is a strong preference to identify as Christian before taking on any ethnic or national identity. First and foremost, they are Christians. This is integral for their self-understanding. It has been a growing trend in the past few years as people derive more meaning from their religious identity than their nationality. That said, they still fill the pull of different national allegiances and live in the tensions between them.

Generally speaking, the Arab-Israeli Christian community wants to integrate better with Israeli society. And there are growing indications that Arab-Israeli Christians are opting to identify with the Jewish state to gain equality while preserving their Christian identity. That said, they are also under much pressure to constantly prove to the Jewish majority that they are not terrorists or double agents subversively trying to undermine and destroy the state. When they criticize Israeli policies, they are often accused of being traitors. Israeli Jews scoff, saying they should be more grateful for the benefits the Israeli state has given them.

They can also get it from the other side, the Muslim community, who accuses them of being Zionists sympathizers due to their associations with the Western Christian world that is supportive of Israel. The main concern for Arab-Israeli Christians is the fear of oppression from Islam, especially with the rise of more radical Islam in the Arab-Israeli Muslim community. Over the last few decades, there has been an increase in sectarian tensions as Muslims have collectively attacked their fellow Christian citizens and vandalized their property. This has happened even in Israeli cities, such as Nazareth. In all cases, there has been no real Israeli police intervention.

The most notorious case was a conflict between Muslims and Christians in Nazareth concerning the building of a mosque in front of the Catholic Basilica of the Annunciation on public land before the visit of Pope John Paul II in the year 2000. In addition to violent attacks, Christians were condemned in the Friday sermons broadcast throughout the city on loudspeakers. As a result, Christians felt deeply betrayed, and many have begun to question where their true loyalty should lie. After so many years of living together peacefully, these events have caused mistrust.

Christians do try to avoid problems and confrontations with their Muslim neighbors. They want peace. But sadly, this peace can be limited to a mere absence of conflict, not the deep peace of brotherly love and companionship. That's their longing as the hidden bridge.

Hearing a Strange Voice

The Mount of the Beatitudes in Galilee is a special place for many Christian pilgrims visiting the land. I recall being there one time, guiding a Catholic priest. After our day of touring, this priest and I went to the pilgrimage house across the Church to have dinner, relax, and get a good night's sleep before visiting our next site in the morning.

Chapter 4

I'll never forget the room where I stayed. It was a single, spartan room. There was no TV, and everything was quiet and clean. I laid down on the bed and dosed off peacefully. The next morning, I woke up very early before the sun rose when it was still dark. Then, out of the dark silence, I heard a voice calling my brother by name and me, "Tony, Andre, Wake Up." The voice was faint but pure. Then right away after that I heard the Muslim morning calls of prayer starting, and as I am writing these words I still sense the fear of the presence of God, the moment I heard Gods voice.

I thought it was strange that it said both of our names, but as we are both together in this business, Twins Tours, and have strong influence on each other as twin brothers, he was also encouraged as I conveyed this for him later. I initially thought the priest was calling us. But I got up and looked around. The priest was in another room far away. I was alone in the room. The next thought that crossed my mind: could this be God asking me to wake up from my spiritual sleep? My heart filled with peace and joy, and I started to pray. Within seconds, I was sure it was him, and I began to praise God for encouraging me and lifting me up again.

Before this, I had always complained to God that I had never heard His voice. I was always somewhat jealous of Mary and Joseph and other people in scripture who had such profound encounters with God. But that morning, God spoke to me. I heard His voice! He gave me that experience to assure me he was with me.

God does not often speak when we expect him to or in ways we anticipate. He can definitely soften our hearts through his Holy Spirit, but that doesn't just happen when we are in our room praying. We can be in a busy place, surrounded by many people, and God can start speaking to us. He often shows up when we are least expecting it. I was definitely not expecting anything that day.

Hearing God's voice that morning inspired me, becoming a turning point in my spiritual walk with Christ. I'll be the first to admit that I had lulled myself into this kind of middle-class-life stupor, taking everything easy and taking God for granted. I had fallen into that subconscious trap of thinking— 'Why do we need God?'—because my life was going well, and I had everything I needed. I had inadvertently been lulled into a very low time in my spiritual walk, and Satan was tempting me with a personal weakness.

One thing I took away from that experience was that I should learn to surrender both the good and bad times to grow closer to Him. I'm so thankful God spoke to me, and I heard his voice that day. It freed me from one of the main weaknesses Satan had been using to tempt me.

God's kingdom is near, and it is at hand. His kingdom is not just in some far-off, distant place. It's OK to enjoy thinking about the future kingdom with God, but we should never do that at the expense of living out salvation right now, in the present. Jesus taught his disciples to pray, "Your kingdom come, your will be done, on earth as it is in heaven."

This was—and is—our invitation to see and experience God's presence today. This is what he taught his disciples in the Sermon on the Mount—and that is precisely what he said in the place right where I was staying. I am convinced we will see God's supernatural intervention in our lives if we decide to give him our priority and make Him our King. We can live in this kingdom today and invite more people to expand the Kingdom of Heaven on earth.

Chapter 4

The Church at the Mount of the Beatitudes

Chapter 5

Christians of the West Bank and Gaza Strip

(The Palestinian Christians)

The theme of the hidden bridge continues. I turn your attention now to the Palestinian Christians of the West Bank and Gaza Strip. These territories became what they are today as a result of the 1948 and 1967 wars, and the impacts they have had on Christians in these areas have been tremendous. But before we get into that, let's start with Jesus and his birth in Bethlehem that ended to be part of the West Bank today.

Background and History of Bethlehem

Geography shapes history, and theology is always related to the physical environment. Bethlehem is in a unique location. The city is on the border between the hill country of the Judean mountains and the wilderness of Judea. That means it receives adequate rainfall for the valuable cropland, while the wilderness nearby also provides accessible pastures for the shepherds' flocks.

Chapter 5

In the first century, the Bethlehem region was occupied by the Roman Empire. Luke, the gospel writer, recounts the historical circumstances of Jesus' birth concerning the broader context of that occupation. At the time of Jesus' birth, the Roman Empire was ruled by Augustus Caesar. He was in power from 30 BC until 14 AD. The governor of Syria was Quirinius, who was in charge at two different times, first between (ten and seven) BC and second between (six and nine) AD.

At the time of Christ, there was much tension in Judea and the Galilee against the Roman occupation. In the first half of the first century before Christ, the Jews revolted five times against the Romans. Four of those five revolts happened because the Romans were contemplating a census that would mean more taxes for the people of Judea and the Galilee. Or possibly conscription into the Roman army.

You may recall from the previous chapter that people fled the cities to avoid the census and taxes until the empire mandated that they return to their city of origin for the counting. This meant that security in the lead-up to—and during—the count would be heightened—Roman soldiers would have been everywhere—and that meant an inevitable and dangerous journey to their city of origin.

To illustrate the perilous circumstances, in six AD, the sons of Judith of Gamla, a Sicarii (zealot), led a revolt. The Romans crucified about 2,000 people in a single day in Jerusalem as a result of that uprising. How would you like to be pregnant Mary traveling through to Jerusalem that day? No thanks.

The census that forced Joseph and Mary to go to Bethlehem was for the purpose of taxation, not conscription. The Gospel of Luke says that the taxation happened under Quirinius the governor of Syria (whom I mentioned above).

If we consider astronomy, seven BC could be a good year for the birth of Christ. There was a conjunction of the planets Jupiter and Saturn that year. The two planets would have been huge in the sky, looking like massive, wandering stars. Perhaps one of these two heavenly bodies was the same one the magi witnessed and followed? At the end of these speculations, we must be humble and realize we will never be entirely sure.

Christians, after all, did not attempt to determine the exact year of Jesus' birth until the fourth century AD. That leaves plenty of room for a margin of error. We know that Herod died in four BC, so Jesus could not have been born in one AD. This is why most scholars today guess that Jesus was more probably born around seven BC.

However, what is clear from scripture is that Joseph had to leave Nazareth and return to Bethlehem for the census, the village of his origin. That was a 120 km journey (approximately 75 miles) to pay the Roman taxes. What is also clear is that God controls history. When Caesar Augustus ordered the census, Joseph had to go to the city where the prophets had prophesied the birth of the Messiah.

But why would Mary go? According to Roman law, only the man was responsible for paying the tax. There was no reason for a pregnant woman to go, especially if she was going to give birth at any moment. The journey would have taken at least a week, which would have been difficult for a woman about to give birth. Given the circumstances of her pregnancy, Mary likely had no desire to remain in Nazareth. Being unmarried, her pregnancy brought dishonor and shame to her family and community and especially now when she is about to give birth.

In the New Testament, you sometimes read the phrase, "Jesus, the son of Mary." But in Arabic and Hebrew, you never say someone was the son of their mother. The father's name is always used—unless of course—there were doubts about who the father really was. Is it possible that speculation about the origins of Jesus' birth persisted throughout his lifetime? We will never know for sure. But we do know Mary chose to take the journey with Joseph.

Now, looking toward Mary and Joseph's arrival in Bethlehem. Bethlehem is located in the center of Judea, and both Joseph and Mary were of the house and lineage of David. He was, after all, Joseph —son of Jacob, son of Matthan, and the son of Eleazer all the way to David. He was of royal blood, a direct descendant of King David. The family of David was famous in Bethlehem. Being from that famous family, Joseph would have been welcomed anywhere in the town.

Moreover, in the first-century culture, any woman about to give birth was given special attention. Rural communities would always assist one of their own in childbirth, regardless of the circumstances. Joseph was returning to his home village, where he believed he could easily find shelter. Could a small Jewish town fail to help a young Jewish mother about to give birth? No way, they would help without question.

But the Bible says Jesus was laid in a manger because there was no room in the inn. That makes it sound like Mary and Joseph had been rejected by the people of Bethlehem. Was that really the case? The answer is no.

First, regarding the inn, English translations of Luke 2 say there was no room in the inn since many people had come to town for the census. But the Greek word *"kataluma"*, often translated as inn, does not mean that—it means guest chamber. A first-century guest chamber was always located in someone's house. That is where guests would eat and sleep in the house. In other words, Mary and Joseph found no place in their relative's guest chambers.

Simple village homes in first-century Palestine often had but two rooms. One was for the family, and the other was for guests. But when there were no guests, the family cow, donkey, and a few sheep would be driven into and housed in that second room. The farmer would keep the animals inside to provide heat in winter and had kept them safe from theft. Those animals would be taken out and tied up in the courtyard the following morning.

The guest chamber would then be cleaned for the day. The door on the lower level served as the entrance for both people and animals. In the Bethlehem area, such homes can be traced from the time of David through to the first century at the time of Jesus. This style of traditional home fits naturally into the birth story of Jesus, and this is how the Arabic-speaking Christian would understand the text.

Christianity in the Middle East has traditionally thought that Jesus's birth would have taken place in a cave. This tradition can be traced back to Justin Martyr, a local historian writing in the middle of the second century. Here's the logic behind the tradition: Many simple homes in traditional villages in the first century began in caves and then expanded. And given the abundance of limestone rocks in that area, hundreds of natural caves would have existed in the slopes in and around Bethlehem.

Second, the Gospels say the baby was laid in a manger. This is a correct translation, but we must still ask: what is implied by a manger? In many countries, the nativity manger is thought of as a wooden cradle stuffed with straw in which the baby Jesus was placed. Mangers were feeding and watering troughs usually carved out of stone. They would be found wherever animals were kept and fed. Their size and shape would be a perfect resting place for a newborn infant.

Chapter 5

A Stone Manger from Tel Megiddo

Newborn human babies are among the weakest newborns on the planet. Many newborn animals can stand within minutes of birth, but not humans. We require our parents to take care of us. God showed us His practical love when He became as feeble as a human baby to give us His Holy Spirit. This is what makes us different than all the rest of His creation. And at the time of Jesus' birth, almost all mangers were in caves. It was one of the best places to be born. Joseph and Mary put the baby in a manger.

To summarize, a part of what Luke tells us about the birth of Jesus is that the holy family traveled to Bethlehem, they were received into a private family home, but there was no room in the family guest chamber, so they went to the house cave where the animals were typically kept. It would naturally be warm and private. After sending the men away, the village midwife and other women would have assisted at the birth. Mary would have only been left alone with the care of the village's women.

Luke also mentions that the child was wrapped in swaddling clothes, and the custom in ancient times was also to be rubbed and cleaned with salt. This is still practiced among village people in the Middle East region. By tradition, a newborn is bathed with salt to keep the bacteria away. After the child was born and wrapped in swaddling clothes, which were long strips of cloth that protected the child from the cold and gave him a feeling of protection. Mary then put her newborn to bed in a manger filled with fresh straw and covered him with a blanket.

Chapter 5

The Shepherd's Different Night

Shortly after Jesus was born, the first proclamation of his birth came to humble, simple shepherds. Shepherds in first-century Palestine were poor, and rabbinic traditions labeled them as unclean. Yet, the first people to hear the message of the birth of Jesus were a group of shepherds who were close to the bottom of the social scale in their society.

Shepherds were considered low people, the outcasts of the community. In biblical times, shepherds were not allowed to enter the temple, and their testimony was not accepted in the court. And because they worked every day, including on Shabbat, they were often accused of breaking the law.

Interestingly, shepherds did not have their own fields in Jesus' day. The fields belonged to the farmers. When farmers reaped their fields, if anything fell from their hands, scripture instructed them to leave it for poor people. That is what enabled the shepherds to get feed for their sheep and goats (there was also a benefit for the farmers, of course, as the animals would naturally fertilize the soil).

You would never see animals in the fields from spring until harvest because they would destroy the crops. They would live close to the desert, where they could forage for their food. Then, after the harvest, they would be permitted to enter the fields and graze.

When the angels announced Jesus' birth to the shepherds, they were told they would find Jesus lying in a manger. This, from my perspective, is the capstone of the story. It shows us that Jesus was born for the likes of shepherds—the poor, the lowly, and the rejected. Jesus also came for the rich, of course. We see an example of this in the wise men who appeared later and brought gifts of gold, frankincense, and myrrh, all valuable commodities in the first century.

But God has a special place in his heart for the poor shepherds as well. They ran to see the child and afterward shared the news around. We see again how God will choose the simple and humble to deliver his message to the world. What a fantastic proclamation for the birth of the child and that the sign of His greatness would be that He was wrapped in swaddling clothes and lying in a manger. Christ used Shepherds to announce and proclaim the good news. Our Savior was not born in a palace but in a manger, and these shepherds obeyed the angels and rejoiced with heaven for the world's salvation had come.

When we hear about the Lord and His salvation, we should first go to Him by prayer and by reading His word until we feel the need to share our joy with our friends. Also, the joy of a new birth stays for the entire life of the parents and family, but Jesus' birth was a joy for the whole world.

Chapter 5

A Cave in the Village of Beit Sahour (The Shepherds Fields area)

The Nativity Church

Before I turn to contemporary Palestinian Christians in Bethlehem and throughout the West Bank, I'd like to share a few brief words about the Church of the Nativity, which was built to commemorate Jesus' birth.

People have believed from at least the second century AD that the specific location of the Church of the Nativity in Bethlehem stands on the site where Jesus was born. One particular cave, over which the first Church was built, is traditionally believed to be the birthplace itself. This place marks the beginnings of Christianity and is one of the holiest spots in Christendom. (Titus 2:11) says, "For the grace of God that brings salvation has appeared to all men."

The Church is also significant because it is the only church in the Holyland that has never been destroyed. When the land was invaded in 614 BC, the Persians set out to destroy all the churches, but they saw a picture of the wise men inside and thought it had to do with their tradition, so they spared the church.

When Muslims occupied the land in the seventh century, they did not destroy it either because they believed in the birth of Christ. Instead of destroying it, they turned part of the church into a mosque. Thus, the church has survived with no significant destruction to this day.

The Nativity Church is more important than the pyramids of Egypt or St. Peter's in Rome. This is the place where Jesus was born, where Christianity started, and where God entered history in an amazing new way. This is our faith and our joy. After all, this is the origin of Christmas.

As you continue to read this book, I encourage you to take some time to look at your life again and allow the God of love to enter His gifts

Chapter 5

into our busy 21st-century lives. We must never forget this moment of incarnation. Consider more ways to make room for the Lord in your lives and share this love that God gave us with everyone around us.

The entrance of the church is a symbol of Christianity throughout all history. When Christianity is the official religion of the land and is not persecuted we see the big square main entrance from the Byzantine period. Later with the Crusaders and Muslims skirmishes we see the smaller Arch Crusader Gate. Whereas at the Turkish period the priest build this small entrance called the gate of humility to make the people leave their animals, bow down in respect before they enter the Church. It is a very unique entrance, and very soon the church will become a museum for tourists that visit from all over the world as we will learn why the Christian community of the West Bank is evaporating!

The entrance to the Nativity Church

Chapter 5

Palestinian Christians of the West Bank and Gaza Strip

In this section, I move forward in history to the present situation of Christians in the West Bank and the Gaza Strip. But before I do that, I have one brief comment about Christmas and the Church of the Nativity today. As you might expect, tourism is Bethlehem's main economic lifeline. Pilgrims are the backbone of the city's economy. They come from all over the world. Every year, a huge celebration happens on Christmas Eve at the Church, commemorating Christmas at midnight mass.

Many Christians today hesitate to attend because more Muslims come from all over the West Bank to participate as a symbol of shared national solidarity. This causes tension with the local Christians, and so to avoid trouble, many prefer now not to show up, choosing instead to celebrate with their families at home.

It's also true that many Christians are moving out of Bethlehem, and it is becoming increasingly Muslim these days. Today, Bethlehem is a Palestinian city of 35,000, primarily Muslim, but with a Christian population of one percent. Although, according to law, the mayor of Bethlehem, whether a male or a female, is always a Palestinian Christian. I share this as a foretaste of the following discussion of the social and political dynamics that inform the lives of Christians in the West Bank and Gaza today. I take each in turn.

The West Bank

To understand the West Bank today, I must first explain how the territory was shaped through the Oslo Accords in the 1990s. An agreement between members of the Palestinian Liberation Organization (PLO) and Israeli government officials, the Oslo

Accords were designed to end the Israeli occupation of Palestinian territories and create an independent Palestinian state alongside Israel.

The Accords established a framework for future negotiations as well a five-year interim period of Palestinian autonomy. They facilitated mutual recognition, brought about the end of terror, and provided a timetable for negotiating the fate of Jerusalem, borders, settlements, and refugees. They recognized the Palestinian Authority in 1995, and it became self-autonomous.

Thus, the West Bank was also divided into three areas. While the full vision of the accords was never realized, some aspects have remained in place. Most significant for our purposes here is the division of land. The Oslo Accords (1993-1995) divided the land into three major zones, A, B, and C. To help you remember them, I've given them three specific names, A-Arabs, B-Between, and C-Chosen.

Zone A (Arabs): The Palestinian Authority has sole jurisdiction and security in this area, but Israel still retains the authority over movement into and out of the area. It allows for Palestinian Arabs to provide their own local security in this zone, which covers only 18% of the West Bank.

Zone B (Between): The Palestinian Authority has civil authority and responsibility for public order, while Israel maintains a security presence and overriding security responsibility. This covers 22% of the West Bank. It is the between area.

Zone C (Chosen): Israeli, for God's chosen people, retains total control of the final 60% of the West Bank. Essentially, this area remains under Jewish occupation where most of the Jewish settlements are located.

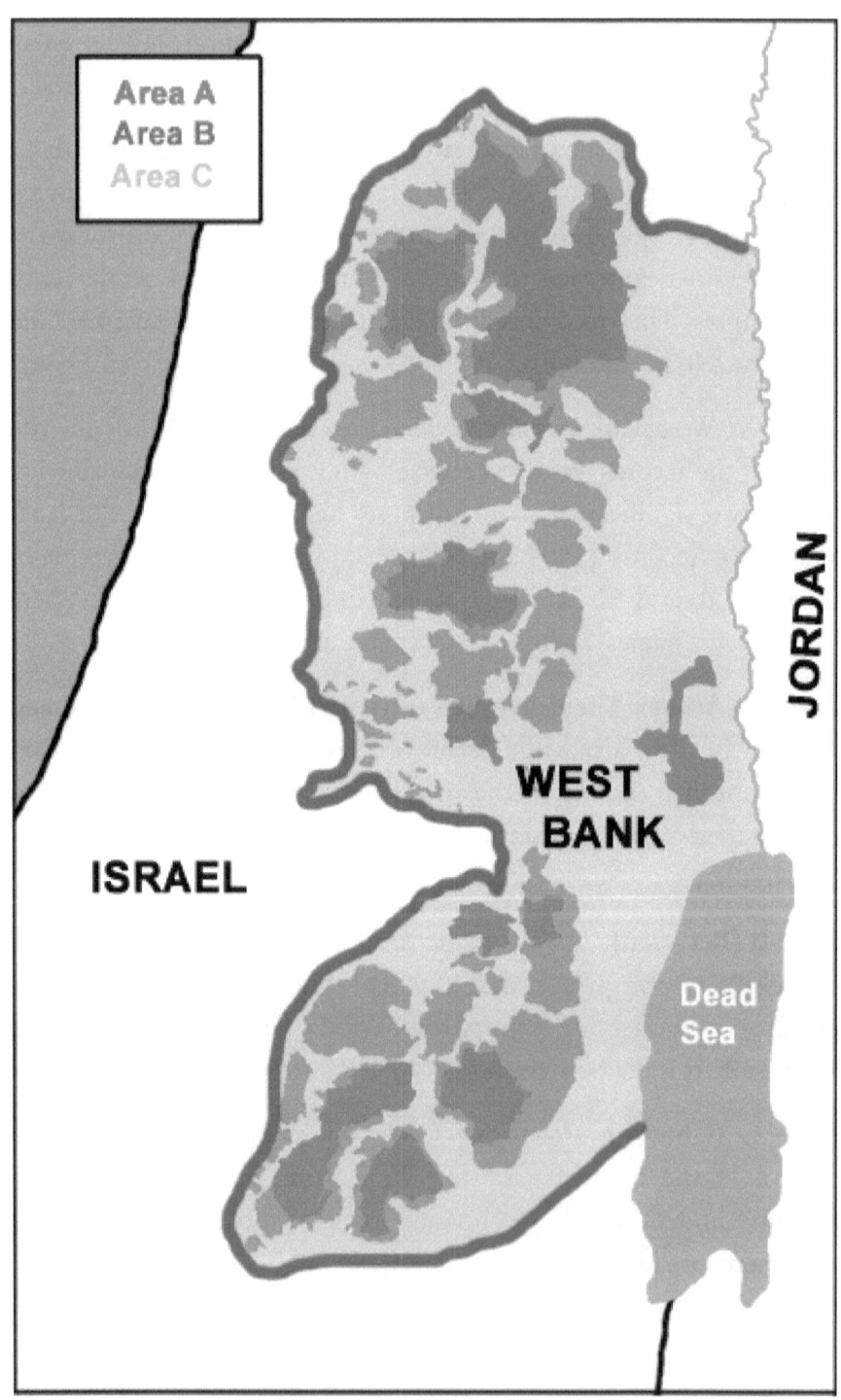

This solution created a need for a system of highways and bypass roads that integrated the settlement blocks into Jerusalem and Israel while creating more barriers for the Palestinians to move between these different zones. The Oslo Accords also made it such that there was no longer free movement between the West Bank and the Gaza Strip, separating Palestinians from one another.

The Palestinian Christians in the West Bank are genuinely suffering. First, they are separated from the Palestinian Christians of Jerusalem and Israel. This breaks my heart. And second, they are persecuted from both sides by the Jews and the Muslims.

Arab Israeli Christians in Israel or the Arab Christians in East Jerusalem face some discrimination, but it is nothing compared to what the Christians of the West Bank face. These Christians are forgotten. And since news outlets or media sources rarely mention them, their suffering goes unnoticed and unchecked.

To start, basic living services are only sometimes provided in the West Bank. Palestinians in the West Bank don't get water regularly since Israel controls the supply into the West Bank. Each family relies on old wells when the water is shut off. And many families have grown accustomed to not having available water throughout the week.

In the Palestinian autonomous areas, Christians do enjoy the protection of the Palestinian Authority. But they are concerned by the lack of democratic structures or laws that force them to accept the rule of the Muslim majority. The majority does not always protect the rights of the minority. Indeed, Christians are the minority everywhere —in school, in the workplace, and in politics. In many places, they are the only Christians.

Remember, only 1% of the West Bank are Christians, and they are mainly concentrated in the area of Bethlehem and its suburban villages. Many villages in the West Bank started as Christian, but they are now primarily Muslim. Nevertheless, the Christians in Palestine are more about quality than quantity. They are a well-engaged minority and are very vocal in advocating justice, developing nonviolent resistance, and promoting reconciliation. Even though our Muslim neighbors accuse us of not contributing enough to the struggle against Israel. They claim Christians are not true Arabs because our religion is western is American!

Also, there are not enough jobs in the West Bank to support everyone. This caused poverty to become a significant problem. Many Palestinians are looking for a way out and are ready to break the law and risk entering Israel to work without a permit, where they can find under-the-table work. Palestinians who work in Israel earn low wages by Israeli standards but higher than laborers in occupied territories. These Palestinians often do manual labor jobs most Jews are not willing to do. These jobs have become a major source of income for many Palestinians.

This situation is similar to what is happening in the United States, where many people from Mexico and Central America sneak across the US border to work jobs many Americans do not want to do, accepting lower wages because they are more than what they can get in their home countries.

During both intifadas (1987-1993); (2000-2004), Palestinian Christians suffered long-term closures and curfews imposed by Israeli armed forces. I personally know of a Christian family from Bethlehem who lives on the main road that ends from Jerusalem to Bethlehem. Their house is next to the boundary wall that Israel erected during this time, zigzagging into Palestinian territory to include Rachel's tomb, a

Jewish site. The main road was barricaded, cutting the lifeline of a once major road.

Muslims would sneak into the Christian neighborhoods to throw stones at and even fire old guns at the Israeli towers guarding Rachel's tomb before running away. There are better spots the Muslims could have chosen, but they deliberately chose the Christian neighborhoods, knowing they were weak and unable to stop them.

Sometimes, they even break into a Christian's home and shoot from that location at the Jewish fortifications. The Israelis shot back with their tanks and sprayed a foul-smelling liquid that lingered for weeks to disperse the crowds. And again, Israel never considered the Christian homes in the middle that suffered from both sides.

The Christians could neither stop the Muslims from shooting from their homes and courtyards nor stop the Jews from retaliating and destroying their homes. Many choose to leave and flee to another country. I can't blame them for doing that, especially those with children.

It reached the point where the Muslims would burn down Christian businesses, and the Christians couldn't even expose who had done it to the authorities, often claiming it was an accident instead. It was simpler to stay silent, accept the loss, and try to rebuild, or their very lives would be in jeopardy.

One time, a truck drove like crazy through a Christian village, a suburb of Bethlehem. The driver, who had come from Hebron, hit cars and people with his vehicle. When he was stopped, he claimed he was mentally ill. But in truth, it was an attack on Christians. This does not happen every day though it comes in cycles and waves.

Given the minority status of Christians and our less developed clan systems compared to Muslims, the Christian ability to achieve justice has been seriously weakened. Matters such as obtaining justice for loved ones killed in road accidents, homes being stolen and then burned so as not to leave any evidence, or even exceptional instances of rape are going unresolved.

The most significant source of concern, however, is even the Muslim theft of Christian land using forged documents. All of this works to benefit the more powerful clans at the expense of the weaker individual Christian families.

Unfortunately, in the last few decades, a more aggressive expression of Islam is gaining a foothold in the West Bank, Gaza, East Jerusalem, and especially in the Muslim cities of Israel. Often, persecution comes because there is an assumption that the Palestinian Christians are followers of a Western religion and that they can only be secret Zionists.

Estimates between the two intifadas claim that about 35% of the Palestinian Christian population has left the West Bank and way more from the Gaza Strip. Emigration among the Palestinian Christians of the West Bank is three times higher than among Muslims.

Mostly, they leave because they do not have opportunities to gain a livelihood or cannot support their families with dignity. We are not ready to steal or earn money illegally. Christians are particularly sensitive to this factor, and the spread of a more assertive Islam is causing more people to leave.

The Islamization of society and the constant suspicion that Christianity is a Western phenomenon is squeezing the West Bank Christians out of the spheres of influence and power, spheres they often helped construct in the first place. As a result, many have chosen to emigrate and live in more unrestricted Christian-dominated regions such as North or South America, Canada, Europe, and even as far as Australia.

Despite all this, Bethlehem remains the center of the Christian thought and interaction with the outside world when tourists make it there. Also, Bethlehem University, Bethlehem Bible School, and many other Christian institutions and Churches have helped develop and sustain the Palestinian Christian presence in the West Bank. Despite these significant challenges and the pressures from both sides, Christians in the West Bank will continue to shine the light of Christ and be the hidden bridge.

THE GAZA STRIP

In ancient times, Gaza was a 5,000-year-old port city, the ancient outpost of Africa, and the door to Asia. The Old City of Gaza was part of the old Via Maris Road that connected Egypt to Mesopotamia. Today, the Gaza Strip is only 25 miles long and between four and eight miles wide, covering an area of 140 square miles. Gaza has the densest population concentration in the world, around 9,000 people per square mile.

Also, the Gaza strip has a very young population, roughly 75% under the age of 25. Out of the total population of more than 2 million, around half a million are refugees or from the families of refugees who were forced to move from areas that became part of Israel in 1948, whereas the rest are the original Gaza people who lived in the Old City and the city center of Gaza. Sunni Muslims are the predominant part of the Palestinian population in the Gaza Strip. That is, 99.99% are Muslims, and only 0.01% are indigenous Palestinian Christians.

The more than two million people in Gaza today have no citizenship, no state, and no freedom. Most of the population has never even traveled outside of Gaza. Gaza is a castrated state; Israel and Egypt control its borders. There are two main border crossings into and out of Gaza, but most of the time, these borders are closed: the southern Rafah crossing into Egypt and the northern Erez crossing into Israel.

After years of Israeli siege and war since 2005, Gaza has become a war zone more than a nation. The high population density and limited land access, lack of sufficient food, military actions, and closures, and economic isolation have affected the health of the population of Gaza.

Starting in 2006, the bitter division and rivalry between Hamas and Fatah led to the Hamas takeover of Gaza in 2007, and their control continues. Recent Israeli governments seem to believe the only way to deal with Gaza is to impose a military solution through highly destructive attacks to strangle the economy and suppress more the majority of its inhabitants.

Since 2007, Israel has imposed a blockade on the Strip that has harmed the economy and caused shortages of basic human needs. Only due to exceptional humanitarian cases are people allowed to pass through the Erez crossing or the Rafah border crossing. So, it is extremely difficult for the Gazans to move even to the West Bank or vice versa. Thus, it has often been called the world's largest open-air prison. Israel has total control of Gaza's shared borders, its coastline, and all the traffic crossing the border. Israel is considered the occupying power and is therefore responsible for the welfare of all the inhabitants of Gaza.

Living conditions in Gaza are terrible. Half of the Gaza population depends on food distributed by the United Nations. The United Nations manages most of the everyday care of the population, from education to distributing food and running medical clinics. Even clean water is scarce. Electricity is out for most people for up to 18 hours a day. Imagine life without electricity in this century where everything we do depends upon it in our modern age.

Unemployment is almost 70%, and those living in poverty are more than 50% of the population. We are not talking about moderate poverty but absolute poverty. With no pumps to take away the sewage, waste floods most streets or is dumped directly into the sea. To compound the problem, their coastal aquafer is becoming salty from the Mediterranean due to the enormous demand on its resource, creating a water shortage.

Pollution from the nearby Israeli industries seeps underground into Gaza; even their agricultural land, about 35% of the area, is located next to the borders. Many times, farmers are not allowed to approach their farmland. Something must be done because this situation is not sustainable.

This distress creates a strong incentive to leave Gaza and enter Israel, but all who attempt to do so place their lives in grave danger. A fence separates Israel from Gaza, and Israeli soldiers are deployed to thwart any attempt to break through the fence and enter Israel.

While Israel almost achieved its goal of stopping the rocket attacks from within Gaza and destroying the tunnels used by Hamas, it has increased the anger and bitterness of the people of Gaza. Their determination to end the occupation and the blockade is growing as they don't have much left to lose. Even more troubling is that people can't speak aloud against Hamas, as they don't have freedom of speech. If you speak against Hamas, you have a big problem.

The situation is only growing worse in the Gaza Strip. It is a major humanitarian crisis. The economy is on the brink of collapse. If no solution can be found, we are looking at a humanitarian disaster of epic proportions. People are frustrated and without hope. For them, there is no light at the end of the tunnel.

So, what about the Christians there today? Gaza has changed drastically in recent years. There are fewer than 800 Palestinian Christians in the whole Gaza Strip who live now only in Gaza City. There are three active churches in Gaza: a Greek Orthodox church, a Roman Catholic church, and a Baptist church—with less than 20 members. The Anglican church, a fourth church in Gaza city, only opens occasionally.

In 2007, just after the Hamas takeover of Gaza, most of the Christian community in Gaza fled to the West Bank and abroad. The rest are stuck in the Gaza Strip. Most have already left, and those who remain are highly oppressed. One of the ways to escape is to appeal to Israel during the holidays to visit their families in the West Bank or to get permission for health concerns to be hospitalized in the Arab hospitals in East Jerusalem. Israel grants special exit permissions for health issues, but once these families arrive in the West Bank, they will not return to Gaza.

They will try to flee through the Allenby border over to Jordan, and from there, they'll go overseas. Israel knows about this, but it will sometimes close its eyes and allow it to happen. I don't blame any Palestinian Christian in the Gaza Strip who wants to leave if the opportunity arrives. If I were living in the West Bank, I would do the same. I can't imagine myself living in Gaza, facing humiliation from both Israel and the Hamas authority.

Furthermore, the Christians in Gaza can't name their children with Western Christian names, like Jack or Johnny, but must choose names used by both Christians and Muslims, like Yousef (Joseph) or Khader (George in Arabic). Christian women chose to wear the *"hijab"* (the Muslim head covering) so as not to be verbally and physically harassed when going to the university, for example. Many Christians are forced to become Muslims, and many who can leave Gaza to the West Bank have not been allowed to return and so haven't seen their family members in years and can't celebrate Christian holidays even with their immediate family.

At one time, the Islamic extremists burned down a hotel when they learned it had served alcohol. Even the Young Men's Christian Association (YMCA) library in Gaza city was bombed in 2008. A Christian can be murdered simply for evangelizing and proclaiming the Christian faith. Another Christian professor who taught at Palestine University in Gaza City was kidnapped and forced to convert to Islam. In Gaza, some Christians give in to fear and intimidation and converted to Islam. But the Christians whose faith is firm, freely surrender their lives for their faith, living without compromise even at the cost of their lives. These Christians prefer to die standing than to live the rest of their lives being hunched over.

One example of this great faith was a worker at a bookshop, one of the staff of the Palestinian Bible Society who attended the Baptist Church in Gaza. He was kidnapped as he was leaving the bookshop and very soon later shot and killed, and this happened during the month of Ramadan, one of the main Muslim holidays. His wife taught her three children to continue to thank God that her husband did not return to them as a Muslim, and her revenge was to pray that the people who had murdered her husband would come to know the Lord!

The darker it gets at night, the brighter the moon shines, but the sun will eventually rise, and the darkness shall flee away. The Christian community is caught in the crossfire. The Palestinian Christians live amid fires, and although fire burns, it also refines. The Palestinian Christians' faith has been refined in the Middle East fires and has made us more aware of God's presence.

Chapter 5

Just as our physical senses are more acute when we are in danger, our spiritual senses seem to become sharper and more sensitive to the supernatural. There is an increased awareness that the presence of the Lord is our joy and strength. Lord, help us to be faithful even in our suffering.

CHRISTIANS OF THE WEST BANK AND GAZA STRIP

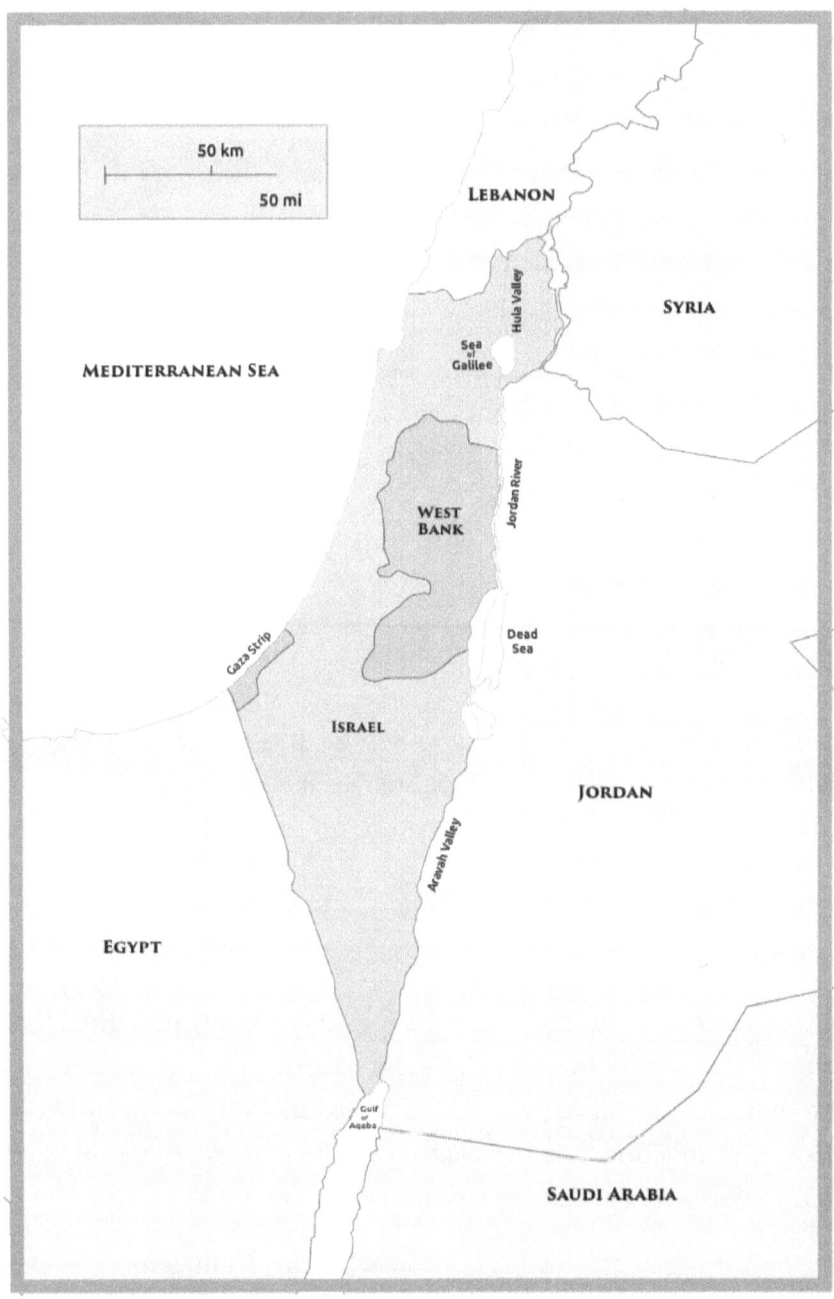

The Holyland Today

CHAPTER 5

STUDYING AT BETHLEHEM UNIVERSITY AND BIBLE COLLEGE

How do I personally relate to the issues and challenges in the West Bank and Gaza Strip? Well, while I was studying at Bethlehem University, my life was changed forever, but I'll get to that in a minute.

My Arabic teacher at Bethlehem University was a religious Muslim, and he treated us Christians badly, mocking us in front of our classmates. Once, he asked me why my name was Tony in front of everyone. He knew I was a Christian, but he wanted to make fun of me. Tony is an obvious Christian name in a Muslim culture. I ended up failing my Arabic class with this teacher as a result of his antagonism.

Another time I was taking my final exams, an Israeli soldier refused to allow me into Bethlehem from Jerusalem. I should note that I was studying in Bethlehem during the Second Intifada (2000-2004). He wanted to know why I was there, telling me to go to Jerusalem to study instead. I explained that I had to go to Bethlehem to take my final exam. I also told him that I was a Christian and that I wasn't going to make any trouble. I only wanted to take the exam, then go back home.

Nonetheless, in my mind, I thought that only a few years before, there weren't any checkpoints at all. Still, he refused to let me in. But I was determined to finish the exam, so I snuck in from the fields. And I wasn't the only one. I prayed that the soldiers wouldn't see me, and I finally managed to get in and take my exam.

But on the way back through the checkpoint, I ran across the same soldier who remembered me. He demanded to know how I got in. I explained that he had left me no choice but to sneak in. I had to take my exam. He detained me for hours, making me wait. He didn't allow me to go until I had talked with a policeman who was a friend of my father's. Finally, I was released in the evening and arrived home safely by the grace of God. These were challenging days.

Growing up in Jerusalem and on into my adult life was a humiliating experience. We often suffered from both sides of the conflict and were not given the chance to express ourselves.

Nevertheless, In my second year at Bethlehem University, my brother and I were invited to a student prayer meeting. At first, we went out of curiosity, not because we wanted to pray. After a few weeks, we were invited to a Christian conference for a few days, and it was there that our lives were shaken. I met people who had joy in the midst of all the trouble around us.

Their lives were real, not fake, and I was convinced of God's mercy. I became a believer as a result of this, and I was baptized in the Jordan River. The last place I expected to become closer to Christ was during my university years. But it was His love that shaped my future afterward.

It was not that my twin brother and I were bad people, I was still searching. It was there that I found what I was looking for. This added meaning to my life, and God is still working on changing me every day. The Alliance Missionary Evangelical Church was literally within a few steps from our home in the Old City of Jerusalem, so my brother and I started to attend (by the way, I still go to this same church with my family). Back then, my family was surprised to see us going to church so often and suddenly.

Then, I attended Bethlehem Bible College, and that's where I decided I wanted to be a tour guide once I finished my education. One of the reasons for my decision was that I was challenged by one of my professors, Dr. Randall Smith. This American teacher knew more than me about the history of my country. It should be *me* who talked about my country, not a stranger.

Another reason for my decision to become a tour guide, was that I met many Palestinian Christians and learned more about their plight. This simply continued to break my heart. At both the Bethlehem university and Bethlehem Bible college, I met some more Palestinian Christians from various parts of the West Bank, even some from the Gaza Strip. Many of the Palestinian Christians in the West Bank area who wanted to find work after they finished their education would leave their villages and come to the bigger cities of Bethlehem or Ramallah for more work opportunities.

Also, a major key event in this period was that I met the girl who would become my wife. The first time I saw her was in the Alliance Missionary Church in the Old City. She'd come up from Haifa, where she lived, to visit her brother who was a pastor in Jerusalem. I inquired after her, but between work and classes, I didn't give her much more thought.

The second time I saw her was while working as the reception manager at the Christ Church guest house in Jaffa Gate while I was a student. She passed through with her brother again. I knew I had seen her before, and she intrigued me, but again, I was too busy working and studying to pursue it.

The third time I saw her was during a Christian conference at Kibbutz Ginosar on the shores of the Sea of Galilee. Almost all the Christians of the land were invited, so Arab-Israeli Christians, Christians from East Jerusalem, and Christians from the West Bank, only those who got a permit by Israel authorities to enter Israel proper, came to this conference. I was finishing up my studies and had started to pray for a wife. I was 27, so it was the right time to be more serious about starting a family.

She kept crossing my path, so I decided to start with her. Through her close girlfriend, that my twin brother knew, I asked for her phone number, which she gave me even after noticing me watching her during the conference. I admit this was a strange move to ask for her phone number through her girlfriend, but I somehow had to jump into the water.

Besides, I didn't know when I would see her again, so I did not want to lose this opportunity. I started talking with her on the phone, and she discovered I was serious about a relationship. Indeed, I wanted to meet her family. And to make the story short, the rest is history, as they say.

God answered my prayer quickly. It was definitely the right time for me! This was the second-best thing that happened in my life after my salvation. The more time passes, the more I am assured she is the right girl for me. She cares so much for our children and me, and she is a huge blessing. Honestly, I can't do this life without her. As of this writing, we have been married for more than 15 years, and she gets prettier each day.

Chapter 6

Christians from Jerusalem

(The Jerusalemite Christians)

In this chapter, like the previous two, I start with a discussion of the background and history of the city, followed by reflections of the hopes and challenges of Christians in the city today. I conclude by offering a bit more of my personal story.

"Thus says the Lord GOD: This is Jerusalem, I have set her in the midst of the nations and the countries all around her." – (Ezekiel 5:5)

Welcome to Jerusalem, a unique city among all cities. Jerusalem is a living, dynamic, and breathing city. The capital of all capitals, it is the most famous city on earth. Though it carries the title "the city of peace," it has been ravaged by centuries of warfare and conflict. The city is sacred to most of humanity: to Jews, Christians, and Muslims.

Although Jerusalem is not as large as London, or as impressive as New York, or as decorated as Rome, or has the population of Tokyo, and has no major river or a harbor on the sea, it is nonetheless the most visited city in the world. Jerusalem is saturated with its royal history that goes back more than 4000 years before the coming of Christ.

Chapter 6

The city is also a spiritual magnet, attracting people from the four corners of the earth, making Jerusalem a mixture of many languages and cultures. To the Jews, it is the incarnation of ancient Israel. Jerusalem has had great leaders and kings, such as King David and King Solomon. It was home to the now destroyed Jewish temple, the place where the Jews worshiped God. To Christians, it is the city where the incarnation of God, Jesus, has spent His last days on earth. And to Muslims, it is the third most sacred city after Mecca and Medina in Saudi Arabia, being the place where the prophet Muhammad in his night journey traveled on his steed from Mecca to the furthest mosque.

Today, Jerusalem is the largest city in Israel. Nearly 10% of the population of Israel lives in Jerusalem. It is 33% Orthodox Jews, 33% secular Jews, 33% Muslim Arabs, and only one percent Christian Arabs. There are less than 10,000 Christians among almost one million people.

Physically, Jerusalem is three different cities: West Jerusalem, which is the Jewish Jerusalem, East Jerusalem, which is the Muslim Jerusalem. And then the Old City in the center, which is divided into four quarters (Jewish, Christian, Armenian and Muslim) and surrounded by ancient walls. While there are no physical borders between East and West Jerusalem, they are culturally divided, and Jerusalem has two centers: the western Jewish Center and the eastern Muslim Center. There is no Christian city center since Christians are such a tiny minority and we are lost in the huge city.

The walls and gates of the Old City of Jerusalem that are visible today are largely the work of Suleiman the Magnificent, the Turkish Sultan who lived in the 16th century AD. These walls have nothing to do with the ancient city of Jerusalem from biblical times—they are merely 400 years old.

The present walls of Jerusalem have 35 towers and eight gates, two on the north, south, west, and east sides. Each gate has a different name depending on if you are Jewish, Christian, or Muslim. The most important two are Jaffa Gate (the main Jewish gate on the west and south) and the Damascus Gate (the main Arab Muslim gate on the north and east).

Besides, the whole city of Jerusalem is built with white limestone. Since the British Mandate, there has been a law on the books stating that the entire city needs to be made out of this special stone taken from quarries around Jerusalem. This is because the British wanted each building to reflect the beauty and grandeur of the Old City. The buildings, old and new, are all made from the famous Jerusalem white limestones, and thus no one can build with any other colored stones.

In the early 19th century, Christians numbered 25% of the population of Jerusalem, around 10,000 people. But this number has stayed relatively the same until today. This means the percentage of Christians in the city, relative to the overall population, has continued to shrink. This small Christian community is bound to the city by religious roots and family ties. Although small in number, the Palestinian Christians of Jerusalem make up an important part of the hidden bridge.

Chapter 6

From Bethpage through the Kidron Brook

Jesus' Triumphal Entry

Let's now follow the first few days of Jesus' last week in Jerusalem. Because Passover was approaching, that meant it was springtime. The first point to mention is Palm Sunday.

A lot of these people have heard about Jesus, and they wanted to see Him, hoping that He would come to this year's Passover in Jerusalem. As you approach Jerusalem, there are three camps for Galileans on the Mount of Olives. There were so many people coming for the Passover that tent cities sprang up on the Mount of Olives.

The population of Jerusalem would grow about ten times more during this holiday. In addition to the camps and tent cities, the villages on the Mount of Olives in the first century, Bethany, Bethpage and Anathoth, also grew in population. Staying inside Jerusalem was expensive at that time, and many of the pilgrims stayed all the way until the next holiday of Pentecost, almost 50 days later.

For several months, Jesus had been talking about going to Jerusalem. Previously, He had always entered quietly. Let us say Jesus came from Jericho on Friday, and then, after spending a quiet Saturday in Bethany, he goes to Jerusalem on Sunday morning. For now, He would enter the city in a high-profile manner. First thing Sunday morning, they walked from Bethany—where he had been staying at the home of his best friends, Mary, Martha, and Lazarus—to Bethpage.

At Bethpage, Jesus sent two of the disciples into the village to get the donkey while He waited conspicuously by the village wall. Bethpage was located at the outer city limits of Jerusalem. Since Jesus was well known in Jerusalem, when the disciples asked for the donkey, saying that the Lord had need of it, the owner gave it gladly.

Chapter 6

But why would Jesus want a donkey? Jewish history helps provide the answer. The Rabbis once discussed how far the bread of thanksgiving could be taken from the temple and still be considered inside the city limits of Jerusalem.

One said you could carry it as far as the court of Israel. Another said you could carry it as far as the court of the Gentiles. Yet another said you could carry it to the city wall. The next rabbi summarized the discussion, explaining that when the temple was standing, the city limits of Jerusalem included Bethpage. This is very important.

Given this, you would expect Matthew, Mark, Luke, and John to say, "They passed Bethpage and reached Jerusalem, and then Jesus sent two disciples to get a donkey and entered Jerusalem riding on it." However, all four gospels say, "When they reached Bethpage, Jesus sent two disciples into Jerusalem." Let me elaborate creatively.

When Jesus reached the black-and-white sign that said "Jerusalem City Limits, elevation 2,700 feet, population 80,000," he leaned on that sign and waited while two disciples went to get the donkey.

In other words, Jesus' request for the donkey was an overt and conspicuous act, different from the way he had behaved in the past. This time, he was going to do something that would make everyone start talking. The famous Galilean rabbi had gotten on a donkey at the city limits sign.

We also have the donkey story because the book of Zechariah in the Hebrew Bible says that the Messiah would come from the east, stand on the Mount of Olives, and judge the nations in the valley of judgment. There is, therefore, an ancient Hebrew tradition that the great King will come from the east.

In Roman society, great kings came from the east. And the Mount of Olives is east of Jerusalem. There is an ancient hope of a great king coming from the east. In fact, many Jews want to be buried on the Mount of Olives to be near where the great king will one day come. The cemetery there is the longest continually used Jewish cemetery in the world, spanning from the first temple to today.

The Jewish Cemetery on the Mount of Olives

Chapter 6

During the last week of His ministry, Jesus deliberately fulfilled messianic prophecies. The triumphal entry into Jerusalem was a dramatic way in which Jesus proclaimed His messiahship, fulfilling in detail the prophecy of (Zechariah 9:9), which says, "Rejoice greatly, O daughter of Zion! Shout, O daughter of Jerusalem! Behold, your king is coming to you, He is just and having salvation, lowly and riding on a donkey, a colt, the foal of a donkey."

And let's not forget the fact that the colt had never been ridden. This was of special significance: objects used for sacred purposes cannot have been used previously for any other reason.

Jesus appeared on a donkey that had never been ridden. Kings come on horses as warriors to fight, but Jesus came in peace on a donkey! Jesus knew these people would return home and talk about the coming of Christ.

So, in the final days of His ministry, Jesus openly declared His messiahship to show His kingly authority. The Messiah is not a secret anymore. This event took place on the Sunday before the crucifixion, which would take place the following Friday.

What happened after Jesus got on the donkey at the city limits? He began riding it into Jerusalem. The people understood what that meant. The people sang hosanna and waved palm branches.

In Matthew, Mark, and Luke, some people brought branches. John clarifies, saying they brought palm branches and sang hosanna, which meant "God deliver us now, please deliver us quickly from the Romans."

The word Hosanna means "save now!" When a Jewish woman calls her son or daughter saying, *"bo"* or *"boi"* in Hebrew, she is saying, "Come here!" When she adds *"na,"* *making the phrase "boina,"* it stresses to come immediately. Essentially, the word 'hosanna' was a plea from an oppressed people to their Savior for immediate deliverance.

The phrase has deep roots in the Jewish tradition. (Psalms 118:25-26) says, "Save now, I pray, O Lord; O Lord, I pray, send now prosperity. Blessed is he who comes in the name of the lord! We have blessed you from the house of the Lord."

Hosanna was a customary shout of praise, like hallelujah. So, when the people were singing it publicly about Jesus, they were acknowledging that he is the Messiah. People expected the Messiah to be a great king, a strong leader, who would deliver Israel from the Romans and return their previous glory.

A king's subjects often pay homage by providing a carpet for the king to walk or ride on. By putting down their clothes for the donkey, they were offering their most valuable possessions to their king, giving Jesus' authority over them.

Jesus had some Pharisee friends (He didn't have many friends who were Sadducees) who said to Jesus, "tell the crowds to keep it down. This is dangerous." Up until this point, being quiet about the Messiah was imperative. But on Palm Sunday, Jesus wanted the people to sing. If they were silent, the stones would cry out. The secret could no longer be kept.

The Pharisees did not want a revolt that would bring the Roman army down on them. But the Lord was not establishing a political kingdom. He was establishing the everlasting spiritual Kingdom of God, and this should make all of us happy.

It was no longer about delivering one nation from the slavery of the Romans but to deliver all the nations from the slavery of sin, welcoming all humanity to the Kingdom of God. There were no more messianic secrets by Palm Sunday.

Chapter 6

The first to hear of Jesus riding on the donkey at the city limits were the Galileans living in the tent cities on the Mount of Olives. Palm branches were symbols of Jewish nationalism, so it was no wonder that Jesus' Pharisee friends told Him to tell the crowds to keep it down.

Today, if you fly the Palestinian flag in Israel, you can be arrested. The colors of that flag are white, red, green, and black. Every Boy Scout troop handkerchief is the color of the Palestinian flag. No one would be arrested for wearing a Boy Scout scarf, but everyone knows what it means.

Likewise, no one would be arrested for riding a donkey, but everyone knew exactly what it meant when Jesus got on the donkey at the wall of Bethpage. No one could be arrested for carrying a palm branch, but everybody knew what it meant. Palm Sunday was a dangerous time. And the Palm branch was a symbol of victory for the Jews.

Jesus wept when He crested the hill and saw Jerusalem, knowing what fate awaited him. There was going to be a terrible war, and the temple was going to be destroyed to show that the Roman god was greater than the Jewish God. The tension could be felt in the air.

It was the Passover, and on many other Passovers, there had been attempts to drive out the Romans. And now there were people waving palm branches and singing hosanna. Passover is when the Jewish people remember that they were freed from Egypt to live in their land, but now they are not free anymore. They are under the yoke of the Romans occupying their land! They would look under every stone for a deliverer.

So, you could feel the tension in Jesus' day, particularly at the Passover. There were extra Roman soldiers on duty. We know of at least half a dozen attempts to revolt against Rome during the first half of the first century. Most of these occurred at Passover.

Several years before Jesus, a self-proclaimed messiah named Theudas of Jordan, gathered a group of people on the Mount of Olives at the Passover holiday. The Romans heard about it and killed him along with four hundred people. They cut off Theudas' head, took it back to the Roman garrison, and put it on the wall facing the temple. This is what the Romans did to anyone wanting to be a deliverer. For Jesus, Pontius Pilate made that perfectly clear on the following Friday. Actually, you did not need to be a prophet to know that war was coming soon. The tension could be felt in the air.

Jesus wanted people to talk about Him in Jerusalem. So, by entering the city as he did, Jesus was leaving this world. The king cried on Jerusalem from the Mount of Olives as He saw Golgotha, the place of His crucifixion. All is becoming real now. Jesus is preparing Himself and His disciples for what was to come. And as if His entry wasn't enough, after he was there, Jesus overturned the money tables in the temple that were being misused. Angry at this, the Sadducees sent their temple guards.

This confirms that Jesus was the humble King. The zealots were looking for a warlike messiah who would use force. Jesus showed a greater power than armed might: the power of humble wisdom and penetrating love. Meekness is not weakness but power under perfect control. I see every Christian in the land here like a little Christ. Our hearts are broken in Jerusalem to bring Christ's love into the hearts of its people.

The authorities were afraid of the crowds. They only got rid of Jesus by taking Jesus at night in a private place when one of His own betrayed Him. They didn't dare arrest Jesus when He was teaching in

Chapter 6

the temple. There would have been a revolt because Jesus was becoming that popular with the crowds.

The power of a crowd may have been the reason why Jesus took a high-profile entry into Jerusalem. Of course, Jesus would not be alive the next week, but His followers would, and the government would be afraid to act against them because of the people's power. People in governmental positions had to be careful. If a procurator could not control the people in his area and they revolted, he would be banished. In 36 AD, there was a riot in Samaria, and Pontius Pilate was banished. There was another riot in 39 AD, and Herod Antipas was banished.

Jesus chose a time when a lot of the Jewish people were present and came from a place where all could see Him. He did this so the Romans would leave Him alone as they were afraid of a revolt, which meant trouble for Pontius Pilate, the Roman procurator. The people thought that their freedom was near, thinking God had given them a king. But their thinking about Jesus was wrong. They ignored His real mission. And when they saw that He would not free them from Rome, they turned against Him.

The Christians of Jerusalem

Our Daily Confrontations

In this section, I should note that since I am a Jerusalemite Christian exemplifying my daily life, it's impossible for me to separate my personal experience from those of my Jerusalemite Christian family, friends, and neighbors. If I switch between discussions of Jerusalemites in general and my specific experiences seamlessly, that's why. I guess you could say I'm caught in the middle...just like every other Jerusalemite.

We Christians in Jerusalem are in the middle, between the Muslims and the Jews. We are also between Palestinians, those who live in the West Bank and the Israeli-Arabs who live in Israel. We are between citizenships, too, and have neither Israeli nor Palestinian citizenship!

Did you catch that? Christians in Jerusalem do not currently have a nationality. But we are not ashamed. As Christians, we carry the message of hope and love. So as a Jerusalem Christian, living between the Jewish and the Muslim majorities and between the Israelis and the Palestinians, our nationality or citizenship is not defined yet!

If they give us Israeli passports and make us like the Arab-Israelis, Jerusalem will become more Jewish—something the Palestinians will not tolerate. Whereas, if they are going to give us Palestinian passports and citizenship, then Jerusalem becomes more Palestinian—something the Jews will not tolerate.

In a sense, we do not belong to anyone. To make it worse, we are not recognized by the world—as if we do not exist. When we want to travel, we get this travel document called "Laisse Passe" that few airports recognize, and it indicates we are of Jordanian nationality!

Chapter 6

This is because Jordan controlled East Jerusalem and the Old City between 1948 and 1967, and so now this designation applies to every resident of East Jerusalem, regardless of when they were born. But we're not Jordanian.

From the positive side, it is a good to be in the middle. As a Christian Arab living in Jerusalem, we can interact with the Palestinians and the Israelis and get to know both sides. Neither the Israelis nor the Palestinians can do that. Thus, we are a very essential part of that hidden bridge that can connect both communities, the Israelis and Palestinians.

Growing up in the Christian Quarter of the Old City of Jerusalem had its own unique challenges. If I walk northeast towards the Damascus Gate, then I will be in the Muslim area of Jerusalem. If I walk southwest to the Jaffa Gate and the new city, then I will be in the Jewish area of Jerusalem, so where do we belong? For as an indigenous Christian, I can look like a Jew if I am in a Jewish area. Or when I am in a Muslim area I can look like a Muslim. In truth, however, I really just want to identify as a Christian and look more like Christ.

I would like to share with you one story among many, that I witnessed personally. The story illustrates the tension between the Jews and the Muslims in Jerusalem. The incident I want to tell you about, is the last one I witnessed while I was an adult, walking inside the Muslim Old City market. I still have the picture of the scene in my mind.

I noticed three religious Muslims, from the way they are dressed, in their forties and fifties walking quickly. As I entered through the Damascus Gate and went into the market of the main bazar, I saw the three religious Muslims approach an Orthodox Jew. I thought at first that they were playing with a friend, but as one person held the Jew with his hand around the man's neck, the other two started stabbing the Orthodox Jew with small pocketknives. Again, nobody dared to interfere else they would be taken to prison and be considered suspects in the attack. Luckily, the Orthodox Jew did not die but suered from light injuries.

It is not wise to be a religious Jew walking alone in the Muslim market of the Old City, even to take a shortcut to the Western Wall. This is radical religion; it blinds people's minds. There is something called the small wall in the heart of the Muslim quarter that radical Jews believe that it is closer to the Holy of Holies than the main western wall. So, few go there to pray.

The police and the Israeli army shut down all the Old City gates immediately to try to catch the person responsible for the stabbing. I don't know if they ever caught him, but luckily the injured man did not die. He was taken to the hospital and eventually recovered.

A Muslim man attacked a Jewish man out of nowhere, and for no good reason. This is radical religion. But it's more than that. Growing up, I always feared the Israeli army, too. I could be stopped while walking home and suspected of some attack at any time just because I was Arab. There was so much violence. But as a Christian, I found my comfort and identity in the church. This is why I have chosen to define myself neither as Israeli or Palestinian but as a Jerusalemite Christian, without any nationality or any citizenship.

This struggle over the land has been long and bitter, but regardless of all that, only the peace of God can prevail. God's values are different from our values. He always uses the unwanted and the minority to forward His Kingdom. A little light can overcome the darkness, and a little salt can change the taste of food for the better. A little hidden bridge can heal big divisions.

Christians in Jerusalem face something akin to discrimination. It is not yet persecution like I described in the West Bank, or in Gaza,

Chapter 6

where you can get killed because of your faith. Because we Jerusalemite Christians are a very small community, we try to mind our own business. But still the Jews and especially the Muslims continue to bother us. They view us Christians as weaker than both. We are peaceful, but both Jews and Muslims don't like to see us happy and joyful. It somehow upsets them to see our families reflecting love, mainly the love of Christ.

Christians from Jerusalem

*The Small Wall in the Muslim Quarter
Entrance near the Chain Gate of the Dome of the Rock*

Chapter 6

When it comes to talking about religion, for example, I can communicate more easily with tourists than I can with my Muslim or Jewish neighbors who I grew up with. This is the strongest evidence for me that our Lord is alive! We have the same Bible and the same Spirit, no matter our differences in culture and language. We find our fulfillment in Jesus, not in politics or in religion like the Jews and the Muslims do.

Here's another story that illustrates the challenges of Jerusalemite Christians. One private Christian school in Jerusalem requested that the religious Muslim girls not wear the "*hijab*" (head covering) on the day of graduation. The principal explained that they had chosen to come to a Christian school and so they should honor Christian traditions. But the school was immediately threatened by the parents, and they forced the principal to submit to them.

The Muslims are more powerful and constantly strongarm the schools into doing what they want. Another difference is that Muslim or Jewish religious schools generally separate the boys and girls, whereas Christian private schools generally do not. One drawback, however, to our Christian education of East Jerusalem is that since it does not follow the Israeli curriculum, we struggle more when we get at the Jewish universities, finding ourselves behind the other students in certain areas.

Another challenge we face is in business. Most of the shops, as an example, in the Christian Quarter of the Old City are owned by Muslims—despite it being named the Christian Quarter. Christians own maybe one percent of the shops. They struggle because Muslims will lower their prices to undercut the Christian shops and drive them out of business. Then turn right around and charge double for fake merchandise when they can get away with it, to make up for the loss. But Christians are not prepared to violate their integrity, and this means suffering. We will never compromise our faith values. This attack on Christians was not so prevalent in my youth, but it is growing more so nowadays.

However, by living in Jerusalem, we also do pay a lot of taxes. More than one-third of our income returns to the government. But at least we can pay our bills and have decent health insurance from the government. And we have clean water to drink, a place to live, and food.

The Hope for Peace

As Christians, we must go forth despite our fear, and only then we will discover more of our faith. The Kingdom is here, but it needs to be manifested. We, as Christians, can leave our mark on society through our Christian universities, hospitals, and organizations, and other areas of service to the community.

We can offer significant contributions to society. But if we fear, we will become isolated and hidden from reality. Hatred cannot be cured by hatred. Love frees us all. Only God's divine love can deliver and liberate us.

Moreover, love seeks justice. We can re-humanize people through love. The future can be changed if the church becomes a peacemaker by spreading forgiveness. We care about all people because the Lord cares for all His creation.

But more so, even when Muslims or Jews hurt us, we still forgive them because our loving God has put His love in our hearts for all people. Without God putting this love in our hearts, it would be difficult for us to forgive our Muslim and Jewish neighbors as they continue harming us.

Chapter 6

Why do they persist in persecuting us? I believe it is our joy that Muslims can't stand, and it is the entitlement the Jews have that makes them feel superior to everyone else. They see the way we live in peace with ourselves! Maybe they will grow upset when they see our love for our families and realize they don't have this kind of love and peace. I also believe it is an issue rooted in spiritual warfare.

We the Holyland Christians have been a witness to the Muslims for many centuries. The West would be wise to listen to us and work through the local Jerusalem mother church and learn from our experience how to be a witness to the Muslims and the Jews.

We have a lot of experience since we have been living for more than a thousand years as a minority. It only takes a little salt to add taste to the meal, and again it only takes a little light to kick out the darkness. So, make use of the little you have. Large gates move and open on very small hinges.

We care for both Muslims and Jews. They are people, part of God's creation. In Christianity, God looks for His people, which is different from other religions where they try to reach a distant God. Christians can pray as a church wherever we are, because *we* are the church.

Every Jew in the whole world prays toward the temple. The Muslims pray towards Mecca. Christians pray directly upward toward God, and this is why many other religions do not understand us. For us, it is more about the spiritual and less about the physical places and directions.

The Jews have to have at least ten people to start praying, and Muslims feel that their prayers are worth more in their mosques, especially on the Friday afternoon prayer. Our prayers do not have to come from a special place or a special kind of position. In Christianity, prayer can come wherever we are and in whatever we are doing. It comes from the heart.

So, during the coronavirus closures, we Christians were the only community that was able to continue praying together because it was not necessary to physically go to church. At the same time, the Jews and the Muslims could not continue their prayers without attending their synagogues and mosques.

Though we Christians are strangers in our own land, nevertheless, we will one day be in our real home, the heavenly Jerusalem. That's where we all belong and will find ourselves close to His presence. This truth gives us the strength to persevere.

But until then, we Christians must be part of the solution, not part of the problem in this land. We will stand strong for the truth and stay fruitful as an olive tree unshaken by any wind that hits us from all directions.

Suffering is part of Christian discipleship, and in our case, that means living alongside the Muslims and Jews. We still have hope and peace in all our circumstances, for to be hopeful is a Gospel perspective. Almost 80% of the persecution of Christians today comes from Islamic countries. Though not all Muslims are potential terrorists, as their nationalism is mixed with their religion.

Indeed, Christian contribution to our society far outweighs the size of our community. Given our higher levels of education and familiarity with the culture of the West, we have provided both the Muslim and Jewish communities with businessmen, politicians, doctors, advocates and theologians. How would the society be different if Christians disappeared?

As the Middle East is tribal and the Christian community is relatively small, it is vital to subsidize it, or we may disappear. With persecution

Chapter 6

and expensive living conditions, many will seek elsewhere to go to raise their families unless the larger picture is understood and the larger Christian world helps.

But on the other hand, this is how Christianity spreads, through suffering. God is in control, and I surrender to this. It is a comfort to be a Christian though we don't belong to anybody here in the land except for God. I don't want to sound over-spiritual, but this truth is what keeps us going. And it is through the troubles that I have grown in the Lord, so I don't want to complain.

To harvest the olives, you need to shake the tree very hard or by striking the branches with a stick. This will not kill the olive tree. On the contrary, it will strengthen its branches. We Christians are like this olive tree. Even when we are persecuted, our core stays pure, and we keep producing oil no matter what happens to us. We know we are under God's protection and in His good hands.

Damascus Gate

Chapter 6

Growing up in Jerusalem

So again, I am a Palestinian but not Muslim. I am Israeli but not Jewish. I am a stranger in my own city. I hold an Israeli identity card but no passport. To travel, I use an Israeli-issued travel permit called *"Laissez- Passer"* with Jordanian nationality. I live in Jerusalem with no official document of my Palestinian national identity. My parents were made strangers to their place of origin. We are indeed strangers in our own city, living in a culture shock. I am a Palestinian Christian with a fragmented identity.

How shall I look at myself? Define myself? Shall I look at myself as a Palestinian Christian living in Jerusalem who is gradually melting into a growing Israeli community? Or shall I regard myself a Palestinian Christian who has no national identity that is recognized by the international community and thus melting into the Muslim society? Only the grace of God can glue together all the broken parts of my identity.

I was born the first of twins to a very simple family. As I grew older and began taking on my firstborn responsibilities, I started to realize how hard my father struggled to provide for four children, me and my twin Andre, as well as our brothers Albert and Alfred. He worked two jobs in his career. His first was as a policeman in the Israeli police force.

This was a difficult career for him. Muslims saw him as a traitor, and Jews never fully trusted him. That meant he was frequently turned down for promotions. Eventually, he decided to quit. But if he had stayed, he would have benefited, receiving a retirement bonus and social benefits for the rest of his life. But to him, that reward was not worth the constant frustrations. So he quit and got nothing of any pension as a civil servant though he served in the Israeli police department for many years of his life.

After that, he worked mornings as a food and beverage accountant in a hotel, and in the evenings, he drove a cab, which meant he did not rest much. He came home between jobs to rest a little, then again after his cab job was done, and then back to work in the morning. This affected his health, and he passed away at a mere fifty-six years old. What I remember most is that he was determined to raise his four boys with dignity.

The year after my father passed, I got married. I wish he had been around at the time, especially when my first son was born shortly thereafter. I named him Joseph to honor him. In the Middle East, the oldest son often names his firstborn son after his father. That's how I was named, too. Tony is my grandfather's name. These are strong family traditions that have been kept for centuries in our communities. My son was a great comfort to me from God after my dad passed away. I see so much of my father in him every day. They have similar physical features and many of the same attitudes.

In the same period when my dad's health was failing, I decided I wanted to start securing my future. To do that, I bought a house on the northern outskirts of Jerusalem in a Muslim village called Bir Nabala. It is much cheaper than buying a house in the city center. Some of my friends in the church already had houses in the same neighborhood, so it seemed like a good idea.

Since I could not afford a house in Jerusalem, the one I bought was slightly outside the city limits. This was no big deal at first. In fact, it was only about a 15-minute drive to the Old City. But when Israel started building the separation barrier, after the second Intifada, the large concrete wall separating Jerusalem from the West Bank, it was no

Chapter 6

longer easy to get to my house. Eventually, I simply ended not going back there anymore.

I only lived one year there when I first got married, but when my first son was born, I decided to move and rent inside Jerusalem to avoid all the suffering of crossing check points to get to work, church, and family. Honestly, I don't know what the future of this house will be, and I don't even want to think about it. I have not been there for many years now. I am not surprised if a Muslim family have simply taken it and someone now moved in to live in my house!

So, we registered our address in Haifa, a Jewish city in Israel where my Arab-Israeli wife is from and where my first boy Joseph was born. Though we, in reality, lived in Jerusalem, our address was not. I know it does not make any sense, but because the home that we bought ended up being on the other side of the wall in the West Bank, it would mean giving up our Israeli Identification and health insurance. To get around it, we registered our address at my mother-in-law's house in Haifa.

This example helps to explain one aspect of Christian family life in Jerusalem that happened because of making a bad decision. I wasn't listening to my Heavenly Father or my earthly father, who advised me not to buy that house that was outside the boundaries of the municipality of Jerusalem.

I put everything I had saved up toward that house because I didn't want to pay rent after I was married. But after only a year of living there, the Jews started to build the wall of separation right down in the middle of the main road, physically cutting it between Israel and Palestine. This wall changed not only the geography but the future of this country by separating this Palestinian village from Jerusalem.

The separation wall is part of what is called the Road Map, designed after the Oslo Peace Accords. It is a complete Jewish-Palestinian maze. Bridges were constructed to cut off Palestinians villages from Jerusalem while tunnels were dug to connect the Jewish cities to Jerusalem. It really does not make sense, but it is our reality.

Even though this road map is obscured, one thing is clear: the wall was built on such a path to exclude as many Palestinian villages on the outskirts of Jerusalem as possible while including as many Jewish settlements as possible into Jerusalem's city limits. In other words, the wall was built for more than security purposes. It had a demographic purpose as well.

Forced to rent a house in Jerusalem, I restarted my family life. But it was the perfect time. Shortly after my marriage, I passed the tour guide exams and finished my studies. A year later, tourism started to pick up, and I was able to start saving some money. I decided that the next house I bought would not be in a Muslim village but in a Jewish neighborhood. I had my eye on a a Jewish place north of Jerusalem called Pisgat Ze'ev inside the Jerusalem's municipality borders.

So, after tourism picked up, and with the help of my family and my twin brother, I was able to make a down payment on a house in that neighborhood. Praise God the bank agreed to give me a 30-year loan. So now I am more stable after what we went through, especially after having grown up in a very small house with low ceilings in the Old City.

In this new house in the Jewish neighborhood, I thought it would be safer than in a Muslim village. But disaster comes when we least expect it. Here's one example: I wanted to install an air-conditioning unit in my new house. I asked for a quote from both a Jewish-owned company and a Muslim-owned company. I knew neither of them. The Muslim price quote was a bit cheaper, so I decided to go with him!

Chapter 6

This took his team almost the whole day to install the air conditioner, which was kind of strange. I did not know what they'd done until almost a month later, when one evening, my family and I went out for dinner. After dinner, we returned home to find our front door slightly open. We immediately thought we had forgotten to shut it. But as soon as we entered, we realized we'd been robbed. This was a real shock. The thieves had entered from the balcony. We could see their footsteps leading to our safe. They'd opened it and had taken all our money and other things of value. I praised God that at least they had not destroyed the house or caused any damage.

In fact, the theft happened after we'd returned from our dream trip to the United States in 2018. If it had happened before, they would have taken our trip money. The Muslims see Christians as weak, so we are a target for them. We reported it to the Israeli police, but years have passed, and we still have no idea if they were ever caught.

The normal everyday type decisions, like installing an air conditioner in our home, costed our family a lot. It is more than the loss of money. It's knowing that someone was watching us until we left our house and then violated our home. I was so glad my kids were not home alone when that happened. They didn't sleep well in their own rooms for the next few weeks.

I forgive those people because this is what God has taught me to do, and hopefully the Israeli authorities will catch them one day. The irony is that I ran from a Muslim neighborhood to a Jewish one, thinking we would be safer, but that was not the case.

It isn't only the Muslims that see us as weak, the Jews do as well. One of my Jewish neighbors who moved into an upstairs apartment installed an air conditioner just above my bedroom window. It wasn't installed well, and it was noisy! It made sleeping very difficult. I tried to get him to move it to another location, tried being polite, tried reasoning. But he didn't care. He dismissed my concerns every time I brought them up. I considered suing him but decided against it. Eventually, I did some retrofitting and kept the windows closed to sleep.

But things got worse. The people who installed the unit had created holes that allowed water to leak inside my bedroom when it rained. I told my Jewish neighbor about this, but he again dismissed my concerns, saying it was only the humidity and I should open my windows. Ugh!

My lawyer said I was crazy for not suing him. He thought I was afraid because he was a Jew, and I am Arab. And there is something to be said for that. If an Arab sues, then he is seen as a bad person, attacking a Jew. And judges almost always take the side of their fellow Jews, so there is a precedent to fear suing a Jew. Regardless, I didn't want to sue because I wanted to do things as a Christian should. I wanted to have a good relationship with him. But sadly, years passed without us talking to each other. But I continued to pray for him.

Then one day, his wife passed away, and I tried to comfort him when I saw him. I could not believe his reaction—He wanted to make things right between us and invited me to come to his house to talk. I was thrilled that this severed relationship was beginning to mend. This change was the result of the love of God.

The bottom line is that Christians in Jerusalem have challenges about where to live. It is not easy for us to live with the Muslims that are becoming more radical. They are not even allowed to interact with the Christians unless they need something from us. Neither is it easy for us to live with the Jews that don't accept us because we are Arabs. For in their Halacha, which is their Rabbinical interpretation, they are not allowed to sell their properties to non-Jews except that I was lucky and bought my house from a secular Jew who did not care about all that.

Chapter 6

Nevertheless, Christians in Jerusalem are in the middle. We have the best opportunity to make a difference as we understand both sides. I try to differentiate between politics and my faith. Politics are important, but they do not constitute my lifestyle as it does for almost every Jew and Muslim in this land. Instead, I try to focus more on the spiritual. Our lives are more valuable than just our physical components. Real happiness is found only in the spiritual and comes from within.

God puts love in my heart for everybody. I could never in my own strength love those who have persecuted me. The pain is too deep, and the offenses too many and too frequent. I am able to love everyone because I constantly experience the love of Jesus, and I can forgive much because God has forgiven me of so much. A servant is not greater than his master. Jesus was tortured and executed for crimes and sins He did not commit, and even while hanging on the cross, He forgave those who had put Him there. I should do no less.

Like your body's immune system, which protects your body from outside harmful elements, the love of God is our mind's immune system. God-given love helps protect you from harmful and destructive attitudes that will eventually weaken and destroy your healthy relationships with others and your Lord.

We are not against any group of people, but we are against the spirit of false religion behind their behavior. In the end, it is spiritual warfare, and our enemies are not flesh and blood. We are against the spirit of religious bigotry. Thus, we should continue to pray for God's love to prevail in their hearts—in the hearts of both the **JEWS** (**J**esus **E**ventually **W**ill **S**ave) and **ISLAM** (**I S**hall **L**ove **A**ll **M**uslims).

I wish that both Jews and Muslims would leave us alone, but unfortunately, the Muslims know that the Christians among them are weak, so they do whatever they want as their religion allows them to do so. They accuse us of being Zionists, whereas the Jews see us only as Arabs and, thus, terrorists. The Jews are so ignorant about Christianity. They think Christian Arabs are Muslims and are even afraid of us at times. I am sharing this with you so that you know how to pray for us and how important it is that the Christians in the Holyland build friendships with you.

Even with all these difficulties, I am glad I was born as a Christian in Jerusalem. My origins are here, and I'm proud of it, and I believe I am called to stay here to be the salt and the light for both Muslims and Jews. So that's my prayer—that people would know the peace of God, and only then can they live in peace together. Christians in Jerusalem are used to being in the middle. That's where they stand on the hidden bridge, bringing the different sides together.

Chapter 6

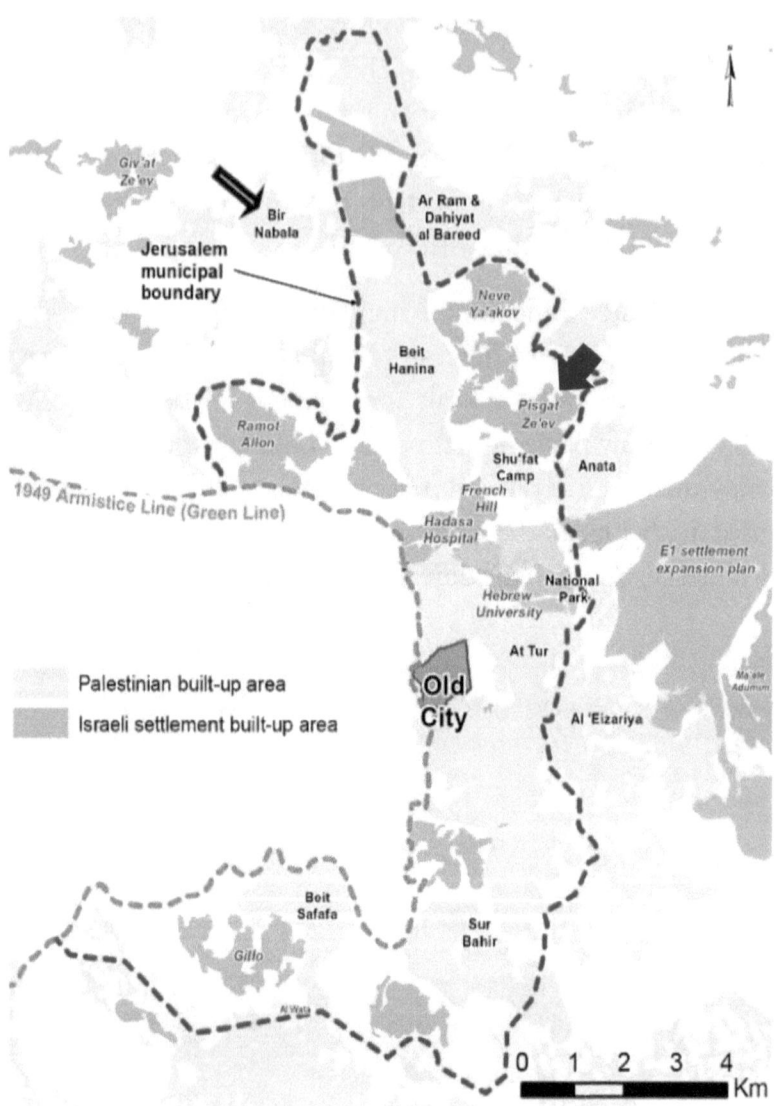

Bir Nabala: the Muslim Palestinian Village
Pisgat Ze'ev: the Jewish Israeli neighborhood

Chapter 7

Christian Believers from a Muslim Background

(The Muslim Background Believers)

In this chapter, I move away from a geographical focus on the different parts of the hidden bridge. Instead, I discuss the Palestinian Muslims who have come to trust Jesus as their Lord and Savior and have, thus, become part of the hidden bridge.

I start with a brief overview of the history of Islam and how this religion became part of the religious and historical landscape of the Holyland.

I then discuss one of my favorite passages of scripture that illustrates how God's great work is often found in the most unlikely of places, which leads into sharing about the experience of Muslim converts. I conclude the chapter by sharing my personal connection to a few of them.

Chapter 7

The Rise of Islam and Arrival in the Holyland

The Founding of Islam

By the sixth and seventh centuries AD, the Byzantine and Persian Empires had been weakened through ongoing conflict on their border regions. This weakening created a vacuum in the Arabian Peninsula where pagan Arab culture was allowed to grow and gain influence, unchecked.

In addition to this vacuum, several other factors allowed for the growth and expansion of Arab culture and influence. Since the Arabian desert had few natural resources that could be developed or cultivated, the Arabs developed nomadic culture and made their living through trade.

Over time, the Arabs became excellent warriors and had highly mobile armies. As their influence grew, local populations throughout the region saw them as their liberators from the Byzantines and the Persians, who had been staging their battles and skirmishes in local towns and villages.

From the perspective of religion, we know little about pre-Islamic Arabia. That said, a few things are very clear. Before Islam, the city of Mecca was small and undeveloped. It was located along the main spice trade route and inhabited by many tribes, of which the Quraysh tribe, dominated trade in Mecca.

We know that the city of Mecca was also a religious center devoted to the worship of the Moon, Sun, and Venus. The moon god was dominant among others, and the crescent moon was a primary symbol associated with the city. Arabian tribes had a custom of traveling to Mecca and worshipping a black rock. Convinced the black rock was holy and should be worshiped, they built a cube called Al-Ka'ba, to house the rock.

Every tribe would bring a small statue of their patron god to the holy rock in the Al-Ka'ba. Mecca was thus a holy site worthy of pilgrimage even before the advent of Islam. It is important to note also that Islam was not practiced before the seventh century, despite the claims of modern Muslims today that Abraham, Moses, and even Jesus were all Muslims.

Also present in the Arabian Peninsula before Islam was founded, were Judaism and Christianity. The pre-Islamic church of the sixth and seventh centuries in Arabia had been weakened through division and the mixing of religion and nationalism. The Byzantine church operated in the Greek language, whereas the Nestorian and Jacobite churches used the Aramaic. Ultimately, the Nestorian and the Jacobite churches that separated from the Greeks under Persian rule extended their reach to most of the Arabian Peninsula, in places like Yemen, Qatar, and Bahrain.

The spread of Christianity among Arabs is evident in the three major Arab Christian tribes, the Lakhmids, the Salihids, and the Ghassanids, who were originally Christian Arabs from Yemen and Hijaz. But due to the lack of communication throughout the region, the moment the Arab Church was ready to crystallize and expand, Islam arose in its place. There are obviously more details to this part of the story, but the main point I want to make here is that there were Christian Arabs before Islam. This is the background and context from which Islam emerges.

Chapter 7

The Life of Muhammad and the beginning of Islam

Islam began as a tribal desert culture and then evolved into an original civilization. Islam is often called one of the world's three great monotheistic faiths. Muslims consider Muhammad to be the seal of the messengers and prophets of God. The religious, social, and political tenets that Muhammad established with the Qur'an, the eternal holy book of their God, became the foundation of Islam and the Muslim world.

Muhammad was born around 570 AD into the respected Quraysh tribe of Mecca in Arabia. His father had died before his birth, and his mother passed away when he was five years old. He was thus brought up as an orphan. First, he was raised by his grandfather, and then later, by his uncle Abu Talib, who took care of him until his death. After that, the son of his uncle Ali Ibn Abi Talib took the responsibility of caring for the boy.

At the age of 25, Muhammad married an elderly and wealthy widow named Khadijah, who ran a camel caravan business. After that, Muhammad began taking care of the business trade and thus earned the title *"al-Amin"*, meaning (the trustworthy).

At 40 years old, Muhammad left home and retreated to a cave, as he was used to do, on Mt. Hira for 40 days, where it is said that he received verbal revelation from the angel Gabriel. This revelation came to be known as the beginning of the revelation of the Qur'an. The angel asked him to read, but Muhammad did not know how, then the angel told him he would guide him in the reading of the true word of God.

In the Muslim tradition, it is believed that the angel Gabriel declared the revelation of God to the prophet Muhammad, one chapter at a time, over a ten-year period. The material itself is affirmed to be both uncreated and eternal in the mind of God. This information wasn't written down yet, only transmitted orally.

When this happened, Muhammad went and told his wife Khadijah about this revelation, and she told him that he had to believe because God had chosen him as his prophet. In time, his authority as a prophet was confirmed by "Waraqah Ibn Naufal", a Christian who was the cousin of Khadijah. They believed God had appointed him as a prophet and thus became the first Muslims.

Muhammad began receiving one revelation after another, and he began to share them openly. His message was primarily about calling people to repent from their wicked ways and worship the one great God. Islam literally means submission to the will of God. Remember that in Arabia at the time, people worshiped many different Gods.

The message of Islam was thus a rebuke of idol worship and paganism and an invitation to return to monotheism. Muhammad's perception of the Christians was that their religion had been corrupted, too, and the messages he received were seen as a correction of that earlier religion.

Soon, more men and women began to accept Muhammad's message in large numbers until the fame of it was spread throughout Mecca. But preaching monotheism to the Quraysh tribes in Mecca was problematic. They felt threatened that they would lose their status and economic advantage as the custodians of the pilgrimage to the Ka'ba, thus the Quraysh tribe began persecuting the new religion.

Other tribes inhabiting the area along the spice route, however, came to listen to Muhammad and convert to Islam. Some 185 miles (around 300 kilometers) north of Mecca was the city of *"Yathrib"*, which is also known as *"Al-Medina"*, (the city). Muhammad moved there because his tribe was not accepting his new religion, while the

CHAPTER 7

people in *"Yathrib"* were more receptive to his message. The people of *"Yathrib"* became known as *"Al-Ansar"*, (the partisans) of Muhammad. The *"Hijra"*, (immigration) ends the period of *"Jahiliya"*, (ignorance) and this marks the beginning of a new era in Islam.

When he arrived in *"Yathrib"*, he proclaimed *"Allahu Akbar"*, meaning (God is greater), the statement that became the mantra for Islam. This move is considered year one in the Muslim calendar when Muhammad became the leader of the city, where the official religion of Islam was born. Year 622 AD thus became the first year of the Muslim calendar.

Muhammad's status changed at this point from being a preacher to a political leader. Before arriving, his revelations and preaching were based completely on theology. Once he arrived in *"Yathrib"*, he became a political leader, almost by default. When people had disputes, they would come to Muhammad for a solution, and he would have revelations and give them a ruling. Muhammad requested to be recognized as the last of the prophets. Governing *"Yathrib"* was a great political victory for him.

It was from "Yathrib" that Muhammad tried to convince three Jewish tribes to join him. After one of the tribes had all the men killed, Muhammad took their women and children as slaves. This made him even more powerful and famous, and Muhammad became the judge of "Yathrib", named later as Al- Medina, meaning literally The City.

With this newfound political power, he wanted to return to Mecca and expand Islam there. Since his own tribe had not initially received him or his message, he returned to wage war and convert them. Shortly after, Muhammad invaded with an army and conquered Mecca. Many believed that such a victory was divinely inspired and duly gave him allegiance. Upon his entrance to the city in 630 AD,

Muhammad went to the Ka'ba and broke all the figurines of Arab gods into pieces. After that, the Ka'ba was Islamized.

From a refugee that fled Mecca to the leader of the new religion, Muhammad became one of the most powerful figures in history. He had denounced the plurality of gods and proclaimed the sole deity of Allah, the one God.

Then, in the year 632 AD, at the age of 62, Muhammad died somewhat unexpectedly. He was in Medina at the time, and he was buried there. He left no clear successor to follow him as leader of the community. His closest followers, *"Al-Sahabeh"*, chose his closest friend Abu Baker Al-Sedik, to become his first Caliph, or successor.

Islam Arrives in the Holyland

After Abu Baker, Omar Ibn Al-Khattab was named the second Caliph. He is known for beginning the process of gathering the materials that would later be codified into the Qur'an. He is also known for consolidating Islam as a religion and a state. He continued the expansion of Islam to the north into Byzantine and Persian territories.

The year 636 AD marked a turning point in the war against the Byzantines. The Muslims fought them in the battle of Yarmouk in Syria and won. The victory allowed Muslims to take great swaths of land and paved the way for them to enter the Holyland and take Jerusalem the following year.

When Omar Ibn El-Khattab entered Jerusalem and took over, he negotiated the conditions of the surrender of the city with Sophronius, the Greek Orthodox Patriarch of Jerusalem and head of the Church of the Holy Sepulcher. Their agreement became known as the covenant of Omar. It ensured the security of the churches and enshrined the obligation of non-Muslims to pay a poll tax to the Muslim state for its patronage and protection. Sophronius offered the keys of the Church of the Holy Sepulcher to the Caliph to honor that place as well. Thus, there was peace between the new Muslims in the city and its Christian residents.

Omar's conquest of Jerusalem is one of the few times in history that the city has changed hands without a battle or any physical destruction to the city. The other important thing that happened when Omar entered Jerusalem was that he was escorted by a Yemenite Jew who had converted to Islam and had traveled with him from Medina. This man helped Omar find the place of the foundation stone while he was looking for the Holy of Holies, and he showed him the famous and holy rock that was atop the old temple site. Omar claimed the rock as the holy site for Muslims, and he built the first mosque there.

The Arabic name for Jerusalem is *"Al-Quds"*, which means (the holy city), where the first mosque was built in that area. Thus, the story of building the mosque is worth telling.

The Dome of the Rock

When Omar Ibn El-Khattab arrived at the famous rock and former foundation of the Jewish temple, the area had been left in disuse for centuries. Nothing had been built there after the temple was destroyed, as the Byzantines left it believing in Jesus' prophecy that the temple will be destroyed. The area remained empty, and the platform was ready for the Muslims to build the *"Haram AL-Sharif"*, which means 'the Noble Sanctuary.'

This Noble Sanctuary is approximately 35 acres (144 Dunams), and it covers almost ten percent of the area of the Old City of Jerusalem today. The complex has been standing since the seventh century, which means it has existed for 15 centuries. That is astounding! Yet, this area is the most controversial place on earth.

Fifty years after the first modest mosque had been constructed, by Omar Ibn El-Khattab, the Omayyad Caliph, 'Abdul Malik Ibn Marwan, ordered the construction of what is today the magnificent Dome of the Rock and his son Al-Walid would complete the project with building Al-Aqsa mosque. The edifice was built between 688-692 AD on the highest spot in the middle of the Noble Sanctuary on what Muslims believe to be the Rock from which the Prophet Muhammad ascended to heaven on his Night Journey.

Muhammad's Night Journey is known in Arabic as *"Al-Isra'",* and its occurrence is recorded in the Qur'an. "Exalted is He who took his Servant Muhammad by night from *"Al-Masjid Al-Haram"* to *"Al-Masjid Al-Aqsa",* whose surroundings we have blessed" *(Qur'an 17:1).* The term *"al-Masjid al-Aqsa"* appears in this verse, and it is the reason the area of the Noble Sanctuary is also known as the al-Aqsa Mosque. The word *"Al-Aqsa"* in Arabic literally means 'the furthest,' and this is a reference to its distance from Mecca. This mosque and two others (one in Mecca and one in Medina) are considered the three most sacred mosques in Islam.

The details of the story of the Prophet's ascent, *"Al-Mia'raj",* however, is only mentioned in the Hadith, the sayings of the prophet. It is said that he ascended to the seven heavens, meeting with all of the main prophets in each heaven—like Moses, David, and Jesus—until he arrived all the way to the top, where he met with God. And there, even the angel Gabriel who had accompanied him on the journey, was not allowed in God's direct presence. Muhammad alone was welcomed, in the Muslim belief.

Chapter 7

With a closed dome and a crescent on top, the Dome of the Rock is the earliest existing model of Islamic architecture in the land. Interestingly, the builders of the dome primarily employed Christian and Persian architects to complete the work (remember, the Arabs were not builders, but people of the desert). To add, 'Abdul Malik Ibn Marwan, the Omayyad Caliph, was afraid Muslims would look to the Church of the Holy Sepulcher, specifically the beautiful dome atop it, and feel inferior. He was afraid it would be magnified in the hearts of Muslims, so he erected the Dome of the Rock with greater splendor.

The Golden Dome of the Rock has eight sides surrounding the supervising Rock. The dome is built around the Holy Rock of Ascension, and the four main sides have doors leading to the inside. From the outside, the lower section is covered with veined marble pieces, whereas the upper section is decorated with polychrome ceramic tiles and geometric and vegetal decorative units.

The golden dome is hemispherical in shape and section. It is covered with gilded copper sheets, and the dome is topped by a golden crescent. Why is it octagonal? First, the Ka'ba in Mecca was square, so they put two squares to give an octagonal shape. Second, an octagon was the best only way to build around the natural bedrock.

On the inside, the natural irregular-shaped rock sits in the center. Its approximate dimensions are 60 feet long by 40 feet wide by 5 Feet High. Some Muslims believe the rock is hanging and suspended. This is because they think the rock did not want to leave the prophet as he ascended to heaven and tried to follow him. But the prophet pushed it back down with his other feet.

There are also several holes on top of the rock, which some believe mark the location of the prophet's footprints from when he was there. These natural rock cuts were more likely used for drainage of the blood of the animal sacrifices that took place on the original altar, the threshing floor of "Arunah," the Hittite.

Below the rock is an almost square-shaped cave where the prophet led all the other prophets of God in prayer. This cave is known as the cave of the spirits, and a large number of Muslims pray inside the cave because they believe their supplications in it will be answered. But according to the Qur'an and the Hadith, there is no importance for this cave written. This tradition was developed later.

Now, having read this background on Islam and its arrival in Jerusalem, you can begin to imagine what a seemingly impossible thing it may be for a Muslim to come to faith in Jesus. But Jesus had a few things to say about seemingly impossible things. One day, he picked up a mustard seed.

Chapter 7

The Dome of the Rock from the Mount of Olives

The Parable of the Mustard Seed

The Word of God is great. The more I think about how great it is, the greater it becomes. One thing I love is that Jesus tells parables in a way to get the audience's attention. The parable of the Mustard Seed is one of those attention-getting illustrations.

> *The kingdom of heaven is like a mustard seed, which a man took and planted in his field. Though it is the smallest of all seeds, yet when it grows, it is the largest of garden plants and becomes a tree, so that the birds come and perch in its branches (Matt. 13:31-32)*

The first thing to say about this parable is that it is very easy to misunderstand. Many people are unaware that mustard plants grow wild everywhere in the Holyland. The mustard plant is one that spreads its golden, yellowish blossoms in the springtime and fills the hills with its color. This is pretty. But if you are trying to cultivate a field so that you produce a crop of something, mustard plants are a nuisance—it is a weed! You try to keep them away from your fields. If you don't know that the mustard plant is a weed, you miss the point. You miss the whole meaning of the parable.

Now, read the parable again, thinking about the fact that mustard plants are weeds. Does that change your perception of God in the parable? The parable hints—or implies—that God is like an ignorant farmer who plants a weed in his garden. Yet, God is not ignorant at all, but He is deeply insightful. Could the Kingdom of God be like a man who plants mustard in his garden? The last thing you want is to allow the mustard to get so big that the birds come and eat the seeds and lodge in its branches. They will destroy your garden.

This knowledge raises a question: what could the point of such a parable be? Surely, God does not consider any person or people as weeds or pests. God loves all of His creation. Could the Kingdom of God be like a farmer who likes weeds or pests? Think of it this way: a mustard seed is very small, and each one is the same shape and size. They are tiny and insignificant. We should not look down on things just because of their size, for they can have greater rewards in the end.

God's word is a seed. Our hearts are the ground. There is life in the seed, let the word grow in our hearts to bear fruits in life. There is a lot of power in the smallest mustard seed. So big things start small, and never underestimate the little you have. It can become big if it is put in the right soil. His Kingdom begins small until it grows and becomes big to change the whole world. Big endings start with small beginnings. Remember, we are all God's creation and made in His image, whether we are local or international, Jewish, Christian, or even Muslim!

Here's another way to say it: God remembers the landless, the refugees, and the marginalized. God does not mind hanging around the people whom society has rejected. If you feel you are alone with Christ, be affirmed that God is building His Kingdom all over the world. He has faithful followers from all over. Little faith can achieve big things.

Faith is a decision rather than an ability, and obedient faith releases the Holy Spirit's power to accomplish the task. His initial limited presence in a small band of original followers will grow to worldwide domination upon Jesus' return.

Let us agree to intercede together in prayer for the salvation of Muslims all over the earth. God, in His mercy, granted the revelation of His Son to all who love truth and who hunger and thirst for righteousness.

The good news is that Muslims are coming to faith in Jesus. They are like little Mustard seeds that are beginning to sprout. No one is a weed in his kingdom, on the contrary the great work God does is through little things as small as the mustard seeds.

The Mustard Plant

Chapter 7

Muslims Who Converted to Christianity

After Islam came to Jerusalem, Muslims ruled the Holyland for almost 1,300 years. With the exception of a brief 90-year period when the Crusaders took control, Muslim sovereignty in the Holyland lasted from 638 AD until the fall of the Ottoman Empire in 1918. Since the time of the first Caliph, fifty-five more Caliphs have followed, extending all the way to 1924, when the last of the Ottoman Caliphs died, and the Ottoman Empire collapsed.

Over the course of Islam's history, the religion expanded greatly to include more than two billion followers today. And they are located all over the world. Today if you are aware 80% of all Muslims in the world are non-Arab; only 20% are ethnically Arab.

Also, according to Islam, it is forbidden for a Muslim to convert to any other religion. The Qur'an says, "And whoever desires other than Islam as religion—never will it be accepted from him, and he, in the Hereafter, will be among the losers" (Qur'an 3:85). This verse and others like it make it very clear that leaving Islam to become a Christian is a grave error.

In fact, a Muslim is not allowed to become a friend with a Christian or anyone who is not a Muslim unless there is a business that must be conducted or there is a benefit behind this relationship. But even then, you are limited in your ability as a Muslim to interact with Christians or Jews to a certain degree.

But the great news is that more Muslims have come to faith in Jesus in the past fifty years throughout the world than in the entire history of Islam. God is doing something great among them, from Morocco to Indonesia. Nevertheless, Muslim conversion to Christianity is fraught with danger.

Christian Believers from a Muslim Background

These former Muslims have the inner conviction and experience to make a big difference in Christianity. Still, it is easy to forget them. They can often be isolated, alone, and marginalized. Their presence is typically hidden because the proclamation of their faith would likely lead to their execution according to traditional Islamic notions of justice. But that isn't the only punishment for converting to Christianity.

They may be tortured in the prisons of their government, or they might be expelled from their homeland. Even if the state turns a blind eye to their apostasy, their family may well take matters into their own hands. It becomes a challenge to keep their faith through the pressure of their own family and friends. Remember, reputation and social pressure are very important in this part of the world.

But the good news is that when they find the truth, they catch fire. It is a shock for them to realize how much in darkness they have lived. After they become Christians and become sure of their faith, they become strong. Many start memorizing the Bible by heart. And they can even challenge Christians who are weak in their faith or who take it for granted. Therefore, many do convert in their hearts but are forced to remain Muslims in relation to their society.

In traditional Islam, there is no separation between religion and state. If they convert to Christianity, they will be estranged. They need to be wise about their hidden faith. Muslims who converted to Christianity face strong resistance in an Islamic state that hears if Muslims have converted or even are invited to convert to Christianity.

These challenges are real in the Palestinian areas of the West Bank and much worse in Gaza, where Islamic Sharia tells them that a convert to Christianity is an apostate—a sin punishable by death. Converting away from Islam is thought to endanger the safety and cohesion of the entire community, and as such, these new believers are often treated as a polluting presence that must be contained, eliminated, or purged.

There is often overwhelming social pressure to force the convert to return to Islam or, failing that, to get rid of the polluting presence of the apostate. A believing husband may be forced to divorce his wife by her family, for example. This can also cause him to lose his inheritance.

Some Muslim converts in the West Bank are forced to leave their homes, villages, and cities and move inside Israel, often illegally, as they are wanted by the Palestinian government, and it isn't safe elsewhere. More so, if employed by a Muslim, the convert will likely lose their job. If their landlord is Muslim, they will likely lose their place of residence, too.

These things are especially true in the West Bank, where there is little legal recourse for those who convert from Islam. In Israel proper, Muslims converted to Christianity are more likely to keep their jobs and houses, as they can remain more-or-less anonymous in the bigger cities.

There are various strategies for achieving these goals for a Christian convert, including keeping the convert confined, forcing the convert to emigrate, or forcing the convert to quietism. The first strategy involves restricting the convert's movements as much as possible to prevent the spread of the contamination. The final form allows for the person to remain but makes sure that their polluting message does not spread.

This represents an agreement not to speak about Jesus or the Christian message and probably an agreement not to attend a local Christian congregation. In the West Bank, the government endangers the church if they accept the Muslim converts. Instead, the Muslim converts to Christianity often form groups called teams or something similar instead of calling them churches. This is not a compromise of their faith but a sensible solution to help keep people safe.

To add, let's say a man from a former Muslim background wishes to marry a girl also from a former Muslim background but who both converted to Christianity. They would need to have two weddings. The Christian one would be secretive, only for the local Christian church. This would be followed by a large Muslim wedding for their families and community. This latter one is the only wedding considered legitimate by Islam.

Add to this in the Muslim tradition, Muslim men are allowed to marry Christian girls so as to bring them to Islam. But Muslim girls are not allowed, in any way, to marry Christian men. This is strictly forbidden. But this may happen with Muslims who converted to Christianity that a former Muslim girl who became a Christian may marry a Christian boy. Few exceptions may happen with the Arab-Israelis in Israel proper, fewer in the Jerusalem communities, but this would almost never happen in the West Bank or Gaza.

The number of Muslims who have converted to Christianity in all of the Holyland is around three hundred. And the number is definitely growing. There are more Muslims who have converted to Christianity now than ever before, and I am not talking about only individuals but whole families!

Another unique problem the Muslim Background Christians face is gaining acceptance and trust from local Churches. They can have doubts about how the local church thinks about them, sometimes seeing themselves as lesser than the rest of the church members. So, it is not easy for them, especially if they develop the wrong idea about Christians being first-class, whereas they are second-class. This is dangerous and can cause more rifts in the local church, separating believers from one another. To get around this challenge, they

Chapter 7

sometimes attend an international church. This makes them feel safer going to a congregation where no one will know them.

From the local church perspective, it is also challenging to welcome converts. It can become dangerous for the Christians as the larger Muslim community could take out their anger on the Christian congregation. On top of this, there is a history of some Muslims pretending to convert in order to take advantage of some of the benefits, like receiving financial help.

They can also come to gather information about the Christians to give to the Muslim religious authorities or even to the government. Such converts start out genuinely enough, but because of the pressures they face, they may revert their loyalties. These things simply make it challenging for a Muslim background Christian to find a church that will accept them.

In one sense, it would be easier and safer for the Muslims who converted to Christianity to not come to the church building itself and risk exposure. But that's not a good solution. To get around this challenge, some churches arrange special meetings for Muslim believers in other safer places and times that are away from the public eye.

I believe Islam is being exposed for what it is, especially from the local Church that knows the Arabic language and culture well. Unfortunately, many Muslims are becoming more radical, trying to defend themselves through terrorism since this is their only means of persuasion. But other ways are failing, and they cannot face the truth anymore. In fact, if Muslims start to think and study more, they will find out and admit that Islam is a counterfeit religion of Judaism and Christianity.

Many Muslims live in denial. They are searching for the truth, as their religion is not satisfying them anymore, and we, the local indigenous Christians, have the answer. Jesus said that He was the way, the truth and the life. The local Christian churches are a little light, and not much light is needed to brighten a dark area. Darkness cannot stand the light, and only then the Muslims will come to life and their eyes are opened to the truth.

The great news today is that so many Muslims want to ask. They want to know. Thank God for the Christian Arab media! They have been broadcasting the Gospel into Muslims' homes. Muslims are hearing the Gospel. And God is preparing a big harvest. Indeed, for many of the Muslims who have believed in Christ, their testimonies have been powerful, especially since satellite channels cannot be controlled.

This is one thing God is doing, but what are we doing? Muslims want the peace we have, but if the harvest dies, the fruit will turn rotten and bring disease and death instead of life. The harvest is great, but the workers are few. The local Christian church is ready and knows what and how to do with the open Muslims that God sends their way.

Converting from Islam to Christianity involves the person of Jesus Christ and God's miraculous involvement in their life. The truth of Jesus' message and the role of the local Christian church believers can give hope and peace to Muslims that is not available to them in Islam.

Converts often feel a great sense of internal emotional and spiritual liberation in discarding Islam for Christ. The challenge to the churches in Israel-Palestine is to be a home where such converts can flourish and help them overcome the other challenges facing the convert, from physical danger to the loss of a job and even much more. As I said at the beginning of this section: God is doing a great thing among Muslims today. The seeds are sprouting and growing!

Chapter 7

Our Church Men's Bible Study

One thing I remind myself of often is that Muslims are people, and we, as Arab Christians, must love all the people of this land, the Jews, the Christians, and the Muslims. God gave us, the local believers, this heart to love the Palestinian Muslims in particular and all the Muslims of the world in general. But we also need to reject the evil spirit of Islam or any other religious evil spirit, be it Jewish or even Christian. The Christian Arabs have a special heart for the people of the land, especially the Muslims. We love them because God loves them. We are all His creation and created in His image.

The local church has learned, through these centuries, how to speak their language and how to connect with them. The local Christian church knows the culture, which is essential in building relationships that will enable us to share Jesus Christ with them.

It is more than just praying that they will accept Christ; it is something that can take years. And then, when someone is converted, there is constant follow-up daily for at least six months until they can get the basics of Christianity. And it is the local Christian church's good fortune to help them go through this transformation because it is a challenging one.

Many bondages must be broken. And this takes a lot of time. Moreover, Islam prevents Muslims from free thinking, threatening violence, and spiritual damnation if they do not follow the precepts laid out for them. They will blindly listen to their leaders. They will be judged if they break community rules. All of these mental strongholds need to be broken down step by step in order for them to be able to think for themselves. And this can only be done by the local, mature, spiritual-filled church that is closest and knows them the most.

The church in the land now knows how to build a healthy relationship with them. Though it is a painful hard process, once they are free and can see the truth clearly, they are so grateful. God has put us here and has given us this responsibility as being Palestinian Christian Arabs!

We are the apostolic church on the front lines of the spiritual war. If the Christians leave, the Holy Spirit leaves too, and then this place will not be an easy place to live. Only more people knowing the Lord can change the land, and this change can affect the whole world.

How beautiful it is to sit together as brothers; it started because of a few of these Christians from a Muslim background that wanted to study the Bible, and now our local church is part of this meeting where we are one in Christ, and we are connected, we focus on the word, and we apply it on our lives.

Every Wednesday evening, my church has a men's Bible study group where we meet in a special kind of secretive room between east and west Jerusalem. The location is in the vicinity of an old church building that is not active. I cannot mention its name, but the room is well-protected and not easy to find.

At that meeting, we truly enjoy sharing together about our past week, laying down some of the burdens of life, struggles, and weaknesses, learning from our failures. We study the Bible, worship, and pray together. The group is led by our amazing Pastor, and no matter how busy he is, he makes this meeting one of his priorities.

Several of our group members are former Muslims who have become Christians, and we share our lives with one another. We hear real stories about their challenges with their families and their work. And they inspire all of us to get stronger in our faith after we see their zeal. They are often the most active ones in sharing their faith with their communities. So that also presents a good challenge for those of us who have been raised in the church.

One activity we have been going now for the past few years is arranging far away outings. These special times together allow us to strengthen our bonds of friendship and point one another toward Christ in a deeper way. I would like to share with you about one of these recent outings.

One afternoon, we got together and drove in a minibus to the northern Negev, and we camped at a Bedouin-style place in the desert with tents, where we had a Bedouin dinner together. After dinner, we sat around a bonfire, when everyone helped prepare, and looked at the beautiful stars in the middle of the night. It felt like God had created this night and this atmosphere that helped us open our hearts more to one another. Our pastors answered some of the hard questions several of us had been facing, and we took advice from each other, listening to one another's experiences that made us all more mature.

Such activities make great memories for everyone. And this one particularly encouraged us to break the ice between us. It didn't matter who was from a Christian or Muslim background. We were all one in Christ, strengthening the bonds between us. We know one another and are connected to one another in a deep way.

One challenge the Muslim guys gave the rest of us from a Christian background was that they said we should memorize the Bible like the Muslims memorize the Qur'an by heart. This challenge made me realize I should become stronger and take my Bible more seriously, and that would give us greater power to evangelize more.

Thus, we all started to know each other more and hear more about each other adventures growing up in the land together through the bad and good times that we had in common. And I could sense the hunger of the Christians that came from a Muslim background for the lord is even way more than the hunger of the Christians of the church. I was so inspired.

This is the hidden bridge—praying together, enjoying fellowship, laughing, going to the desert, and talking about Jesus around the fire. And to top it off, we went on a Camel ride in the desert the next morning and had more time to laugh and reflect. It is through experiences like this that the different parts of the hidden bridge are being strengthened.

CHAPTER 8

CHRISTIAN BELIEVERS FROM A JEWISH BACKGROUND
(THE MESSIANIC JEWS)

THE FINAL PART OF THE HIDDEN BRIDGE IS ESSENTIAL—

the Jews who have come to follow Jesus. We know that salvation history began with the Jews, and, to this day, God is still doing great work among them. Like the previous chapters, I have organized material around history and scripture in the first part of the chapter. The Jewish history is a wellspring of knowledge that energizes faith.

The second half of this chapter is about the present situation of the Jews who have believed in Jesus for their salvation. This group, as you likely know, is often referred to as the Messianic Jews. I look at their faith and their challenges. I conclude the chapter by sharing about my Jewish mentor, a man who himself is a hidden bridge.

THE THREE PHASES OF THE JEWISH HISTORY

As we first look into Jewish history, one of the great realities is that so much of the history is recorded in the Bible. By looking at Jewish history, we begin to understand God and God's character, how He has worked,

Chapter 8

and revealed himself to humanity. I will look at three phases of Jewish history: 1) the Old Testament period, 2) the Jesus period and what happened with the Jews, and 3) the western shift from the Jewish roots.

The Old Testament Period

From the very beginning of scripture, we get an idea of who God is. God is the creator of all things. His power is infinite, and when he makes things, they turn out good. God is loving, and He puts within creation the ability to respond to him in loving gratitude and worship. Humankind is made in God's image and that further affirms God's goodness.

But as you know, the connection between God and man was lost quickly. We humans chose our own path and rebelled. God had to break off the relationship because he was simply too good, too pure, too great—too holy to be in the presence of sin. Nevertheless, right after that fateful fall, God began to make a way for the restoration of the relationship.

God began to make covenants, understandings between him and his people—that they could return to his presence under certain conditions. The first covenants were with Noah, Abraham, Isaac, and Jacob, and they specifically focused on their belief in the one God. There were no further demands on the Patriarchs except belief in the only one God, the Creator of all.

Yet this was nearly unheard of in a culture that was full of many smaller gods: the moon god, the sun god, the river god, the mountain gods, and so on, worshiping the powers of nature. God is one. After time passed, the sons of Jacob, Abraham's great-grandchildren, ended up living in Egypt together with their brother Joseph.

Great events took place for the Jewish nation in Egypt and during their return under the leadership of Moses and Aaron. These events demonstrate God's power to redeem and provide for His people. The pivotal event was the giving of the Torah, with basic codes of conduct between God and man and then between man and man in the Ten Commandments.

But when the people chose to worship a golden calf instead of God, the concept of sin and punishment for sin, were clarified and further developed. The covenant was established through 613 commandments in the wilderness, and many of them involved the construction of the tabernacle that became God's dwelling place.

The covenant under Moses before the Jordan crossing demonstrated the power of God and the benefits of steadfastness in the covenant. After they entered the promised land under the leadership of Joshua, a great event took place at Shechem (present-day Nablus in the West Bank located between Mount Ebal and Mount Gerizim): where the Israelites had been instructed to pronounce the blessings and the curses of the law.

The intent of the covenant was to establish that God was the only God, and that Israel was God's people. Moses and Aaron had established a plan to maintain steadfastness with the covenant and its promises, using daily and weekly rituals locally, and later annual pilgrimages took place at the tabernacle at Shiloh for the appointed times set by God. But the influence of neighboring Gentiles and their false gods was strong, and the result of outside influence eroded trust in God.

God allowed other people to dominate the land of Israel as the Hebrews violated the covenant. God sent judges to repeatedly bring the people back to Him through miraculous victories over their oppressors. The victories returned the people to God in a declaration of renewed faith expressed by sacrifices and worship.

As the Hebrews started to see the city-state systems around them, they demanded that God give them a King, like the other nations. God then sent the prophet Samuel to lead the people and to anoint kings. But under King Saul's disobedience, God punished Israel. Then the obedient King David overcame Israel's enemies, rebuilt the tabernacle, and established Jerusalem as the new center of worship.

I like to think of the material we have covered so far in terms of three markers:

God began His plan by calling **Abraham**. He is the **first marker**. Abraham was equivalent to the high priest since he was the one who left his homeland and began the worship of the one true and unseen God.

Moses was the **second marker** in Jewish history. He received the Torah at Sinai and handed it down to the generations following. So, he was considered a prophet of the Jewish people who communicated with God on their behalf.

The **third marker** in Jewish history was **King David**. David established the beginning of the great kingdom of Israel by uniting all the tribes and bringing the ark of the covenant to the city of Jerusalem. God was preparing the world for the coming Messiah. Starting with Abraham, then Moses, who delivered the Jewish people and moving on down to David.

Picking up with Solomon, David's son, he built the first stone temple in Jerusalem, ending all local sacrifice and concentrating a centralized place of worship in Jerusalem at specific appointed times. Later, in punishment for Solomon's excesses, Israel was divided into northern and southern nations. The northern kingdom of Israel struggled with idolatry, while the southern kingdom of Judah occasionally had good kings.

Finally, due to their continued disobedience, God allowed the northern kingdom of Israel to be conquered by the Assyrian Empire. In time, the Babylonians conquered the southern kingdom of Judah because of their idolatry. The Babylonians destroyed the first temple that was built by King Solomon. Although the Hebrew nation found themselves in exile, God had given them a promise that they would one day return.

Nehemiah was the leader who, with Persian help, brought the Jewish people back from exile. He also led the reconstruction of Jerusalem. Ezra, the scribe, rebuilt the sanctuary (Temple) and read the Torah to the people, banishing idolatry and instituting the learning of scriptures. Leadership was formed under the Chief Priest, known in Hebrew as the *"Cohen Ha-Gadol"*. Judah then enjoyed religious independence under Persia and Alexander the Great. The great assembly, known as the *"Kennest HaGedolah"*, was founded as the Jewish court and parliament.

As people studied the scriptures, they began to notice that the prophets pointed toward a coming Messiah and the afterlife. Yet divisions emerged within the priestly class of those who perform the rituals. Eventually, the Sadducees, known as the *"Tzudkim"*, and the Pharisees, known as the *"Purshim"*, took separate paths. Judaism thus emerged in two parts: the Sadducees, who served in the temple and performed the rituals, and the Pharisees, who taught and preached in the synagogues of every community. The Sanhedrin court was formed for the first time under the shared control of Sadducees and Pharisees.

The Jewish people then had a time when they were free from idolatry. But they soon returned to their wicked ways, and God, as a result, allowed a struggle to break out between them and the Seleucid Greeks

Chapter 8

that would ultimately last a century. One effect of the struggle was that it caused some Jews to leave the land and scatter themselves in a diaspora.

The struggle also brought in Hellenistic influence and religious oppression began to have an impact on those in the temple and those steeped in the Torah. Eventually, priestly Hasmoneans ignited the first revolt in the second century BC. Matityahu and his sons liberated all of Judah from Greek control.

Diaspora Jews who had been scattered during the Greek oppression began joining the pilgrimages coming to the land. Under the Hasmonean kings, Judeans established hundreds of settlements in Galilee, Pereia, and Golan: in the northern part of the land. Meanwhile, the Edomites and Sidonians: in the southern part of the land were forced to convert to Judaism or be banished.

The Jewish Hasmoneans invited Roman control in 63 BC, then Herod constructed a massive temple complex. Hundreds of thousands of pilgrims came to Jerusalem to learn and worship. At the time, rules began to surface in the interpretations of the oral law. And the division within the priestly class became very stark. The Sadducees were aristocratic, priestly, and wealthy through Roman cooperation. The Pharisees were preachers and teachers, often travelers and poor.

More divisions developed during this time. A group known as the Essenes came into existence. They were Aaronic priests who loathed the wealthy Jerusalem priestly elite. They are famous today for writing the Dead Sea Scrolls, which were found in Qumran shortly before the modern State of Israel was established. The Zealots were another group who armed themselves and preached that violence was the way to rid Judea of Roman control and establish the Kingdom of Israel. Among them were the Sicarii, extreme Zealots who often assassinated collaborators. This is the period in which Jesus of Nazareth was born.

Christian Believers from a Jewish Background

The Western Wall in Jerusalem

Chapter 8

The Jesus Period and what Happened with the Jews

Then, at this point during the Roman period, humanity was ready for the manifestation of the love of God in a new and powerful way—Jesus Christ, the Jewish boy from Nazareth, came. He was the fulfillment of the three markers I mentioned previously: He is our High Priest as Abraham was, our Prophet as Moses was, and our King as David was! He came to rescue his people—all people—from the darkness and sin that had become so pervasive.

Since I have already covered so many great details of Jesus' life in previous chapters, I'll only quickly note that the history of the church began on the day of Pentecost (Acts 2). The church was born in Jerusalem and quickly spread to the Western pagan Roman world through the ministry of the disciples and the early believers. Jesus' disciples themselves then raised up disciples of their own, teaching them all that God had commanded, specifically that Jesus was the Messiah and that He had poured out His Spirit and blessings upon these men. Persecution broke out, but this only fueled the fire of the Gospel, spreading it across the world.

One of the great persecutors was Paul of Tarsus, a Pharisee. He had a divine encounter with Jesus and eventually became the greatest evangelist, church planter, and writer of many books of our New Testament today. The Apostle Paul, along with his friends, made three courageous trips to establish churches in many different countries.

However, the Apostle Paul had great success in winning over God-fearing men, both Jews, and Gentiles. Those who regularly attended the synagogue, who worshiped their God, and who studied Jewish scriptures were the ones Paul had the greatest success in turning them into believers in Jesus and in becoming his own disciples.

Christian Believers from a Jewish Background

As Paul spread the good news about Jesus through the known world, many Jewish believers—of whom there were tens of thousands—remained part of the commonwealth of Israel. They continued worshiping as Jews and going to the temple. They continued to be part of Jewish life.

Simultaneously, great growth among non-Jewish Gentile believers in Jesus happened under the teaching of Peter as well. Thus, over the first century of the church existence, the church became culturally and religiously mixed with Roman and Greek culture. The nucleus remained Jewish, but the number of Gentile converts who came from the Roman world continued to expand.

But then, forty years after Jesus' resurrection and ascension, the main second Jewish revolt broke out in 66 AD against Roman rule. One interesting thing about this point in history is that the Jewish believers in Jesus refused to take part in the revolt. Instead, they fled east across the Jordan river to what is today called the Hashemite Kingdom of Jordan.

Within a few years, the Roman army surrounded Jerusalem and destroyed the Jewish temple in the year 70 AD that was built by Herod the great. Suddenly, there was no more temple for sacrifices and no more place to go for pilgrimages. This was the first real breach between the Jews and the Jewish Christians, that is the first Judeo-Christians.

After the destruction of the second temple, one particular rabbi by the name of Yohannan Ben Zakkai survived. He, along with others, formed a new council of the Sanhedrin Jewish court. This began what we know of today as rabbinic Judaism. The group set specific religious and legal standards for Jews that continue until today. These standards contrasted starkly with the values and opinions of the

Jewish followers of Jesus. One might even argue they were developed as a critical response to Christianity.

When the new council later discovered that a few followers of Jesus were still worshiping in the synagogues and had refused to join the revolts, they passed a ruling that all who believed in Jesus as Christ were cursed. This effectively excluded Jewish believers in Jesus from the synagogues.

Led by their rabbis, the Pharisees developed a new form of Judaism that could exist without a temple, a place for central worship, or where pilgrimages were not needed. It focused on prayer and study to keep the people together, so they went deeper into the oral law. This prompted the Pharisee rabbis to begin writing down the Oral Torah and recording how best to be obedient to God's Sinai commandments.

The Oral Torah became more formalized and was observed universally in the diaspora. Community prayer began to take shape based on the liturgy of the Psalms, which Levite choirs had once sung in the temple. The prayer included supplication for redemption, asking for deliverance from oppression, a downplay of hope for a Messiah, and prayers against oppression and rebuilding of the temple. Practicing Judaism became, essentially, a life that strictly followed the Torah commandments that were unrelated to a central place of worship.

Around 130 AD, a man named *"Bar Kochba"* meaning (the son of the star), was declared by the great rabbi Akiva to be the Messiah of Israel, and he rose to prominence. His ascendence sparked another revolt against Rome. This was the third major Jewish revolt, and this time, there was condemnation and active rejection of the followers of Jesus because they refused to fight in this war as well. The believers rejected Bar Kochba as the Messiah, choosing instead to believe that *"Yeshua"* was the real Messiah. The Romans responded to the revolt by casting all Jews out of Jerusalem.

In 200 AD, Rabbi Yehudah Hanassi, head of Sanhedrin, completed the Mishnah, a collection of Oral Torah rulings in Hebrew that included detailed accounts of sanctuary life for later generations. Thus, the Hebrew Canon was set.

The Western Shift

A very strong wedge was driven between the Christian church and the Jewish synagogue at the beginning of the fourth century. There came the final change to this relationship when the Christian church merged with the Roman state, and the Roman Emperor Constantine officially made Christianity the state religion. After this, masses of Romans came into Christianity through baptism and communion in the year 313 AD.

Shortly after, in 325 AD, at a council called by Constantine, the church very explicitly decided upon the separation from anything Jewish. The church leaders began teaching that God was no longer dealing with the physical Israel but the spiritual Israel, the Gentile church. The forces behind this decision were complex, covering the spectrum of political, social, and religious issues. In fact, Jewish believers were totally forbidden to attend a synagogue service.

Over time, the church then began taking on distinctly Christian rituals and festivals, such as Christmas, a change that would further alienate Jews from the possibility of considering the teachings of Jesus.

In 391 AD, the Sanhedrin was abolished by Byzantine Emperor Theodosius II. He did not want the Jews to have a central leadership. He also doubled the taxes for anyone who refused to become a baptized Christian.

In 400 AD, the *"Gemara"* (completion) was added to the Oral Law in the Mishnah to create the Jerusalem Talmud, which was produced in Galilee and in Golan. Judaism thus began to take shape and was developed strongly between 100–400 AD with the formation of the Talmud.

Afterwards, the Roman-Byzantine taxation led many of the Jews to move to Persian Babylon, and around 500 AD, the Babylonian Talmud was written. It was based on the Jerusalem Talmud but with adjustments to the Oral Torah life in exile.

In summary, Jewish believers were prevalent throughout the first century after Christ. But antagonism developed between Rabbinic Judaism and Christianity, which led to fewer and fewer Jews having the opportunity to hear the good news of Jesus. Meanwhile, the geographic center of Christianity shifted to the Roman empire in the West, and Christianity primarily became a faith of non-Jews. But God was not done with the Jews. Centuries later, something miraculous would begin to happen.

The Parable of the Lost Sheep

Before I talk about the miraculous growth of the Messianic movement, I would like to pause and reflect on one parable that reveals the character of God in a beautiful way, especially as it relates to God's love for his lost children. The parable of the Lost Sheep (Luke 15:1-7).

To understand the parable, you need some background on shepherds and sheep. Shepherds primarily kept their flocks on the fringe of the wilderness during winter and led them into the cooler mountains during summer. Usually, adult Bedouin males delegated the care of flocks to young boys and girls. The children would learn this responsibility from early childhood. And they could be in the fields tending the flocks several days' travel from home.

Shepherding was difficult. They faced burning sun and cold winds. Regardless of the conditions, they were responsible for the care of their sheep. Sometimes, a shepherd had a donkey that carried him and his provisions. At other times, he simply walked. A camel-haired coat and a simple head cloth protected him from sunburn while he stayed with the flock.

This covering helped keep his sweat from evaporating, allowing a breeze to cool his body in the hot desert. It would help keep them warm at night, too. The shepherd would eat what he carried with him: dates, figs, olives, and bread. The sheep provided meat, wool, and, most importantly, money, as they were sometimes sold for sacrifices at the temple in Jerusalem. Bears, lions, wolves, and other predators lived in the wilderness areas in the first century.

At night, shepherds put their flocks in a sheepfold, in a nearby cave or pen, or in an enclosure in the wilderness.

Chapter 8

The Lifestyle of Shepherds and Sheep

Sometimes, the shepherd slept across the opening of the sheepfold, acting as a gate to protect the sheep and prevent them from straying. Shepherds would use stones to close the entrance of the cave, leaving enough room for one person to stay at the door. This person was literally called the door shepherd. At night, the shepherds would bring their flocks inside the cave to protect them from predators and robbers.

Interestingly, shepherds of different flocks often shared the same cave, taking shifts staying awake to guard the sheep. During the night, the herds mingle, but that is not a problem. In the morning, the first shepherd would come and use a special call or whistle to beckon only his flock. His sheep would hear his voice and go out rejoicing. This is followed by the other shepherds. Only the sheep who know their master's voice follow. The shepherd and the sheep knew each other well.

But even if a sheep got confused, the shepherd knew every sheep by name. If he saw a strange sheep, he could direct it to where it belonged. Though sheep are feeble and weak, they have very strong hearing and know their shepherd's voice. They can't see well and easily get lost. They can only see the back feet of the other sheep; this is why they follow each other. So, they rely upon their hearing more than sight. Without their shepherd, they easily get lost.

The availability of water was and still is the most important thing for survival in the desert. Yet floods in the desert occurred unexpectedly. The sky would be clear, the sun shining, and suddenly a wall of water could roar through the narrow canyon. Anyone unfortunate enough to be in a *"Wadi"*, (a dry river bed) could be washed away. Yet these raging waters often left behind refreshing pools, and it was the task of the shepherd to determine if they were safe and quiet waters.

So, a significant part of the shepherd's life was finding water for the sheep. Sheep lacked discernment and would sometimes choose dangerous water. That is why the shepherd had to lead the sheep. The good shepherd knew the safe and dangerous times to enter a *"Wadi"*, and he knew where to find quiet pools. Knowledge of both was essential to ensure the flock's survival.

So, when shepherds find safe water for their flocks, they often mingle together. Then, when a shepherd was ready to leave, all he had to do was shout or whistle, and amazingly, his flock of sheep would come to him. Sheep followed only the shepherd they recognized, ignoring all strangers. A simple call from their shepherd was sufficient for an entire flock to follow his lead. The shepherd scouted for new green pastures, quiet water, and places free of danger.

Shepherds pastured their sheep on barren hillsides unsuitable for farming along steep canyons. Visitors to the near East often wonder how sheep find anything to eat on those hillsides. Yet, shepherds knew that small tufts of grass, watered by occasional rains or moist breezes, grew along the edges of the rocks. These barren hillsides were, where the green pastures shepherds in biblical times led their sheep to. The shepherd had to be aware of steep canyons and difficult paths as he led his flock to green pastures and quiet water.

The Parable

Why would Jesus use such a parable? Let's imagine a lost sheep. If the shepherd took time to take the flock to someone else to watch over them, then the lost sheep would only become further lost. So, this parable shows how valuable and important the individual is to God. The care and concern of a shepherd illustrate God's love and serve as an example of the mutual care that we should practice. God is concerned with one lost person and rejoices in his recovery. That's how we should be, too.

Lost sheep lie down helplessly and refuse to budge. The shepherd knows he must rescue them, or they will die. That's why the shepherd rejoices when he finds the lost sheep. God takes care of every single soul He creates. It sounds foolish for a shepherd to leave the 99 and go looking for one lost, but the love of God is so great that He looks for every single one and is happy when He finds it. And surely, we see how much God values every human who is made in His image.

Faith comes from hearing. We also must learn to live by faith, and God will direct us to know His will in our lives if we listen to His voice. We do not have to struggle with what to do next. Jesus is the Good Shepherd and will direct us, like a loving shepherd who cares for his flocks. Even the defenseless are secure in His tender care.

This is the secret of satisfaction: the Lord is my shepherd I shall not want. What I have in God is greater than what I have or don't have in life. The sheep is the least able to take care of itself. They always need a shepherd to lead them. The shepherd is in charge. The shepherd selects the trail and prepares the pasture. The sheep's job—our job—is to listen and follow their shepherd.

Jesus is in front, clearing the path and cutting the brush. Showing the way. He leads us. He tells us what we need to know when we need to know it. Since His provision is timely, I can enjoy the present. He seeks new fields with no companion other than His sheep and no desire other than their welfare. He leads them to the deep grass of the hillsides.

Sheep get hurt, thorns prick, or rocks cut them. This is why the shepherd regularly inspects his sheep, searching for cuts and abrasions. He doesn't want the cut to worsen. He doesn't want today's wound to become tomorrow's infection. To be healed, the sheep must stand still, lower their heads, and let the shepherd do his work and pour the olive oil on their wounds. The sheep do not understand how the oil heals. But they *do* know that healing happens in the presence of the shepherd.

While Jesus walked on earth, most of his followers were Jewish. But this changed as time passed, and Judaism passed through the transformations I discussed above. Yet, in recent years, some Jews have begun to recognize his voice again, the voice of the good shepherd calling his sheep by name. They have been lost, and Jesus is doing everything possible to find them.

The Messianic Jews

Today, the typical Jewish understanding of Jesus is that he was a first-century rabbi who taught outside the boundary of Judaism. Many Jews don't even know the name "*Yeshua'*", Jesus' Hebrew name, which means salvation. Instead, his name has been shortened to "*Yeshu*", an acronym that means (may his name and memory be blotted out). The name "*Yeshu*" by itself has no meaning in Hebrew and allows the average Jew to avoid the truth of Jesus as salvation.

Generally speaking, most Israeli Jews today are ignorant about the New Testament since they do not live in close proximity to Christians. They also know little about Christianity since they have a strong Jewish identity which precludes anything but the Old Testament.

Christianity can make Jews uncomfortable. Christianity reads the Old Testament through the lens of the New Testament, which gives a very different view than Judaism. They believe that Judaism is for Jews. And they are not eager to welcome converts into the covenant given to the children of Abraham and Sarah, although they accept converts on occasion.

They are not comfortable with faith conversations outside of Judaism either, thinking Judaism is superior to all other religions and people, especially to that of Christianity. They can feel threatened by a Christian's attempts at evangelism. Yet some Jews have come to believe in Jesus, and they are called Messianic Jews.

The origins of the Messianic community can be traced back to the Christian missions to the Jews that began in the 19th and early 20th centuries. Messianic Jews in Mandatory Palestine were part and parcel of the protestant missionary organizations located in central towns like Jerusalem, Jaffa, Haifa, Safed, and Tiberias. The Jewish believers in *"Yeshua"*, (the Hebrew name for Jesus), had a strong desire to prevent their total social, cultural, and theological assimilation within Gentile circles.

When Israel was founded in 1948, only a handful of Israeli Jews believed Jesus was the Messiah. By the 1960s and 70s, Messianic Judaism was gaining popularity, known by many as "the Jesus people", and eventually "Jews for Jesus." The movement experienced further growth in the 1990s. By the turn of the millennium, leaders estimated that there were between 5,000 and 7,000 Messianic believers scattered in some 80 congregations and house fellowships throughout the land of Israel.

Today, the number of Messianic Jews in Israel is estimated at around 10,000- 15,000, with over half being Russian speaking, though there is no way to verify this number. Twenty years ago, a Jewish believer was a very rare thing. And even now, more than half of them emigrated to Israel and were not born in the land.

Chapter 8

The Messianic Jewish community in Israel now comprises several generations, with approximately 40% of its members native-born Israelis, and others mainly from the United States, Latin America, Russia, Ethiopia, and other countries. Messianic Jews go through the Israeli education system, serve in the army, often achieving significant responsibilities and recognition, play active roles in society, and are becoming more visible and accepted in all walks of life. They have their own community institutions including schools, theological colleges, and communal support mechanisms.

This community has tried to straddle the line between Judaism and Christianity. Just as they believe Jesus is the Messiah and that he died for the world's sins, they also believe that the Jews are the chosen people and that the explicit laws of the Torah such as observing Shabbat, holidays, and circumcision, must be obeyed today.

The term Messianic Jew is one of several titles by which Jews who have come to believe in Jesus as the Messiah describe themselves. Over the centuries, Jews who embraced Jesus have called themselves Nazarenes, Hebrew-Christians, Jewish-Christians, and Jewish believers. The Modern Messianic Jewish Movement describes the larger community of Jewish people in recent days who have embraced Jesus and continue to self-identify as Jews.

Because Messianic Jews identify with Jesus, all the major denominations of Judaism (Orthodox, Conservative, Reform, and Reconstructionist) have rejected Messianic Judaism. The state of Israel does not recognize Jews who believe in Christ as the Messiah as Jews. In some sense, they must choose between being Jewish or Christian, as they cannot be recognized as messianic Jews according to Israeli law.

Nevertheless, Messianic Jews are ardent Zionists because of Israel's centrality in God's plan. They support Israel because the Jewish State is viewed as a direct fulfillment of biblical prophecy. Although Israel is far from perfect, Messianic Jews believe that God is active in the history of the nation and that the Jews will never be driven out of their land again. While God may love the Arabs, he gave the Holyland to his chosen people, Israel.

Messianic Jews thus seek an authentic expression of Jewish life, maintaining substantial communal ties with the broader Jewish tradition while simultaneously being energized by the belief that *"Yeshua"* of Nazareth is the promised Messiah.

For an example, today, the Messianic Jews drop the word *"knessiah"*, (church) and use instead terms like *kehillah* (assembly). Also, they meet on Saturdays instead of Sundays. Keeping the Jewish Sabbath has a special significance to Messianic Jews. Sunday observance is treated as unbiblical. Messianic Jews almost unanimously believe that the Passover should be celebrated according to the Jewish calendar. And keeping the Jewish sabbath and feasts expressed the central and authentic Hebraic-Jewish national features of their faith.

Therefore, they don't call themselves Christians but rather refer to themselves as Messianic Jews. They reject the use of the Hebrew term *"Notzri"* (Christian), wishing to express their connection to Judaism and clarifying that they are still Jewish, which is a huge deal since Judaism would call any Messianic Jew a *"Notzri"* and thus view them as no longer Jewish.

Their unwillingness to take on the Christian label can cause tension between them and the Christian church over the land. This prevents the relationship between the two groups from growing beyond a certain point, even though we are all one body in Christ. Other differences also contribute to the tensions.

Chapter 8

The Challenges of Messianic Jews

Let me start this section with a disclaimer: Messianic Jews experience multiple challenges with their own people in Israel. They are often discriminated against and persecuted by their fellow Jews. In this respect, they can have a very difficult time. I have heard some heartbreaking stories. That said, since I am an outsider, I hesitate to share details about their own internal challenge.

Likewise, I do not want you to get the impression that I have real authority on this topic when I simply do not. If you would like to know more about that topic, I encourage you to seek out other resources. The knowledge and authority I do possess, however, is to speak about the challenges that come up between the Messianic community and their Arab brothers and sisters in Christ.

A very sensitive challenge exists in the relationship between Messianic Jews and the Arab Christians of the land. And it is often tense with unresolved theological problems related to the role of the State of Israel in God's plan of salvation, a situation that is exacerbated by ongoing conflict between Jews and the Palestinian Christians. The rebirth of Israel is a clear fulfilment of prophecy, and a first step in God's plan towards her ultimate salvation and restoration, but only when she repents and receives Christ, mainly in the Tribulation.

How can we function and work together as one body in Christ for the sake of this country and provide an example of coexistence in a land where such cooperation is rare? The answer must begin with open, honest communication. Unfortunately, this kind of unity has become even more difficult as the communities are becoming more isolated from one another due to the restrictions on travel and the separation barrier erected during the Second Intifada.

Currently, Israeli Jews are forbidden by the Israeli government from entering areas under Palestinian control, and Palestinians are not allowed to enter Israel either. This leaves Palestinian Christians living in Jerusalem and Israel with the most opportunities because interactions are not inhibited legally and physically.

Given this, it is a massive undertaking to simply connect Palestinian Christian and Messianic churches, particularly between West Bank Christians and Messianic believers. There must be unity, but that will likely never happen until the physical barriers between Israel and Palestine are torn down. In addition to the physical and legal barriers, several additional factors contribute to an almost nonexistent relationship.

Here are some of the main ones: The issue of the land and the creation of the State of Israel fulfilled prophecy, the Messianic commitment to their Jewish identity, the cultural differences and low prioritization of the relationship and the high percentage of Messianic Jews being new immigrants.

The exaggerated centrality of this theological position is aggravated by the fact that Messianic Jews often draw political implications from it. Messianic Jews tend to be more right-wing in their political views. If the regathering of the exiles is a prophetic fulfillment, there could be a purpose to that action beyond just fulfilling prophecy. Thus, their eschatological concerns can outweigh issues of social justice. It is important to note that the issue is more than their theological beliefs. The issue is the predominance of these beliefs for many Messianic Jews.

Moreover, there could be fear and concern about being open and public about Messianic convictions. They thus hesitate to publicly acknowledge their religious and spiritual connection to Christianity.

Chapter 8

As a result, they are very cautious when relating to their Christian Palestinian brothers and sisters.

Interestingly, however, most Arab Christians can sympathize with their Jewish brothers and sisters in this way. They understand the difficulties they face from their own people, just as Christian Arabs face similar challenges with their Muslim neighbors. Yet Messianic Jews do not manifest the same level of understanding toward their Arab brothers and sisters.

While it is true that, in some respects, Messianic Jews share a similar faith to the Christian Palestinian Arabs, the hard truth is that this shared faith does not unify enough when it comes to the issue of the land and the State of Israel.

They tend to have little understanding of the people who have their own story and history in the Holyland, a story which most Messianic Jews seem to avoid. They have precious little sympathy for a nation and people who have largely been expelled from their own land and have lost their freedom to live in dignity.

This story is not over, and these wounds are still open. I am sad when I find that my Jewish brothers value the land more than other human beings and more than their belief in Jesus. And despite their shared faith in Christ, some Messianic Jews may believe it would be better if there were fewer Arabs, who they see as problematic from a security standpoint as well.

What is to be done?

More joint prayer meetings, conferences, and study days between these two groups would help. This would connect us in other relational ways that would promote peace and unity. Open and frank talks between the pastors about the theology of the land and prophecies that might be related to Israel would help, even if they were not easy.

Our Messianic Jewish brothers and sisters should hear our story, and they should hear what happened to our people, our land, and our villages. I suggest this not simply to make them feel guilty but to help them understand the gravity and sensitivity of this subject for us, the Palestinian Christian Arabs.

Unfortunately, the general feeling is that such dialogue would likely harm relations even further. Since the relationships are already tense, dialogue would need to begin with basic beliefs and shared values common to both groups.

Both sides should be mature enough not to let this subject damage their relationships. Therefore, the first and most important step is to let the love of Christ overwhelm and fill all our hearts. Christianity is unique over other religions of Judaism and Islam with that love that God poured into our hearts.

Sadly, I must admit that our churches are reaping what we have sown. We do not communicate the importance of this relationship to our congregations, and, as a result, we are raising a whole generation that does not value a relationship with their Jewish brothers and sisters in Christ. Indeed, many Palestinian Christians from the West Bank have difficulties trying to reach out to people who are seen to be the reason for their suffering. They feel they are usually the ones expected to make compromises and sacrifices, not the Messianic Jews.

All these challenges build walls in people's hearts and minds. This is especially true when so many of the Messianic Jews newly emigrate to Israel. The general feeling is that these immigrants don't really understand the story of their Arab Christian brothers, so it becomes frustrating to try and educate them. Generally, we are not believed and are held in suspicion.

Although the Christian Palestinian Arabs are a very small minority, we are aware that we belong to a larger family around the world. However, we find it disappointing when we feel that our brothers and sisters in Christ are not aware of our existence.

And it is frustrating when we discover that these brothers and sisters often fully support the Messianic Jews at our expense. Why is the Jewish part of the body of Christ cared for more by Christians abroad? Are Christian Palestinian Arabs somehow inferior and the Jews somehow more important?

Since we are one body, then improving both the Messianic and the Christian Palestinian Arab relationship is essential to have a healthy life. You need the two lungs to breathe and to be healthy. You can live with one lung, but you will struggle. So, the feelings of being neglected by the greater Christian community results in bitterness and distance toward the Messianic Jews.

The only solution is to listen to each other and express the desire to have a relationship built on Christ's love. To have a healthy relationship, we need to be open and transparent with each other. The relationship between the two groups is extremely important since this relationship is vital to expressing the unity of the body of Christ to the rest of the land.

When this happens, it will be possible to pray for each other genuinely, to be part of each other's ministry, and to serve and care for one another. The love of Christ has the power to overcome all haters, prejudice, greed, and misunderstanding. I am convinced that through Christ, we will be able.

My Mentor, a Messianic Jewish Pastor

Mentors change people's lives. And one of my closest mentors has been a messianic Jew. As a mentor, he was patient, brave, and hardworking. I could go on and on about his virtuous characteristics. He has always seen me as a part of something greater, and he has helped me envision how to manage my future better, revealing new layers and possibilities that I had not considered before.

During the time of our focused mentoring, we would meet regularly. Sometimes at his office, in a coffee shop, and even over Zoom. He was able to see and understand my situation well and give advice about what I should do in the future to make it better.

He specifically gave me very great tips, especially for my business career and how to better manage things during crises. He had a profound impact on helping me keep my head above the water and take a breath before sinking back into the middle of any specific challenge. He was especially helpful during these changes of the Covid pandemic that the whole world passed through.

He showed me how to invest wisely during the hard times to bring good out of it. For example, he helped me develop passive income by doing virtual tours and made my guiding business career extend far beyond my current circumstances.

I am now more confident in the direction I should take and encouraged to obtain my goals. He also helped me realize what was missing to succeed more in my professional life. In short, he taught me how to react to obstacles and to stay motivated, having a solid career direction in this ever-changing world.

Despite the challenges and theological differences between Christian Palestinian Arabs and the messianic community, my mentor and I

CHAPTER 8

have formed a deep bond of trust. I refuse to let the larger challenges prevent me from forming these meaningful relations. I do not share this story to boast in myself; rather, I share it because it is a pure expression of the hidden bridge, the way of Jesus that can connect and redeem all people.

Part Three

The Hidden Bridge Revealed

Chapter 9. The Christian Arab Theology

Chapter 10. The Parable of the Good Samaritan

Part Three

The Hidden Bridge at Mount Carmel

Chapter 9

The Christian Arab Theology

In this final part of the book, I turn my attention to two areas where I see the hidden bridge being revealed. One way is broader in nature and involves the development of Palestinian Christian Theology as a meaningful response to the current challenges Christians face. The other is narrower and aimed at practical and personal application. It's about living out the Christian life as Jesus taught through the parable of the Good Samaritan. In both cases, my aim is to encourage you and invite you into a deeper engagement with the issues from a theological and practical perspective.

The Emergence of Palestinian Christian Theology

Christianity began in the Middle East. And from this land, Christianity launched the Good News of Jesus to all nations. Christianity was not imported from the West. Jesus was not baptized in the Mississippi River, nor He was tested in the Nevada desert in the

Chapter 9

United States. In fact, from our land here Christianity was exported to the West.

Our country, our history, our geography, everything here in the Holyland speaks Christianity. Christianity was born and took shape in the Middle East. The previous chapters have already testified to this fact. We must cherish this truth and convey it to our Christian friends in the West.

Now, let's take a step back and ask: what does the hidden bridge look like when you put all the parts together? What emerges when we combine biblical history and geography with the hopes and challenges of Christians throughout the land? What might it look like to read the Bible from a Christian Arab point of view, through the local Palestinian Christian eyes?

In previous chapters, I shared the historical background of specific places and biblical insights that emerge from understanding the languages and cultures of the Middle East. I will not repeat that material here. What I want to do here is focus on the primary theological challenge the Arab Christians have faced and how we have gone about addressing it, namely, the establishment of the state of Israel.

When Israel was established in 1948, tremors of enormous magnitude shook the very foundations of Palestinian Christian beliefs. We Christians have been exposed to a religion, Judaism, that transformed into a nationalism called Zionism and promoted a version of basic human rights on a religious basis. But did their human rights include us?

More, we Arab Christians are well aware that the West generally connects the establishment of the State of Israel with the fulfillment of Biblical promises. And frankly, this is something we do not understand. How the physical land is more important than the Christian spiritual life! For Christ should be our ultimate goal, and not anything else. We always considered the Bible to be for us. But now, since the establishment of Israel, the Bible was no longer a consoling or encouraging message but a frightening word.

Somehow, my salvation—and that of the entire world—were no longer the main concern of the Bible. The main issue transformed into the land; a land that had been promised to the Jewish people. And that meant I no longer had a right to live in it—because I am not Jewish?

Speaking personally, the God I had known since childhood, the God I knew to be loving, had suddenly become a God who confiscated land, waged wars, and destroyed people. I began to seriously doubt a God who seemingly preferred one group of people over others. I needed to find a new way to read and understand the Bible, so I could define my identity in biblical terms and not as being the enemy of Israel.

What I wanted to know was: how can the Bible, which had apparently become a part of the problem, become a part of the solution? How can we read the Bible in light of this conflict? The Old Testament has given legitimacy to the State of Israel, giving them the right to be here in our land. Thus, Palestinian Christian theologians have tried to find solutions to this problem. Here are some of their suggested solutions:

One suggestion is to reject the Old Testament. Simply instruct Palestinian Christians to read the New Testament only. If we do that, the logic goes, we won't have any problems. There is no direct mention of the election of the Jews in the New Testament, and none of the authors speak about the Promised Land in terms of the Jews needing to return to it for God's divine plan to be fulfilled.

Chapter 9

The problem is, of course, that this is only one way of looking at the New Testament. And we cannot give up part of the Bible. The Bible includes both the Old and New Testaments. This is a suggestion no Christian theologian can accept.

Another suggestion is that we should replace the name of Israel in the Scriptures. So, whenever the term comes up, we could replace it with another one, such as "the people of God." I understand why some Palestinians would lean toward this suggestion. We do not want people, especially those in the West, to confuse biblical Israel for the modern State of Israel.

To us, these are two very different things. But replacing every instance of a word in scripture is a radical idea. And not using the name of Israel in the scriptures only creates new problems. That suggestion does not work either. Palestinian Christians should read the Bible as it was written, with the name of Israel included.

A third suggestion is to offer a new view of biblical hermeneutics, a more liberal way of reading and understanding the Bible. This approach would take many of the Old Testament events as mere myths. With this path, God could be loving without forcing us to deal with conquering and killing of the Old Testament in any meaningful way. Of course, this solution is also unrealistic. Our God is not a God of myths or made-up stories. We believe the entire book is the Word of God.

So then, if every one of these suggestions is problematic, what then is the solution? Before you continue reading, I want to ask you to refresh yourself, pray for the Spirit of God to work in your heart, be open to new things, and allow God to make changes in your mind and thus, in your soul.

The Christian Arab Theology

I need to make two quick points before I proceed. First, to understand Palestinian Christian Theology on the subjects of Israel and the Land, it is helpful to know the historical environment in which these topics emerged as focuses for Palestinian Christians. Second, you need to know that serious reflection on these issues only really began in the late 1980s. The Church in the Holyland is growing more mature due to the rich communication that is developing in our century, which did not exist before.

But why did Palestinian Christian theology develop so late? If the theological crisis between the biblical land of Israel and the modern State of Israel has been around for centuries, we could expect to find this problem addressed, for example, in the Balfour declaration in the 1940s.

We could also expect to see Palestinian theologians writing about these issues shortly after 1948 or even in 1967. But nothing was written until much later. Yes, a lot was written in the 1960s and 1970s by pro-Israel theologians from the West, but nothing by Arabs, not until the 1980s.

The reason is that the conflict did not begin as a theological crisis for Palestinians. In the beginning, the conflict caused more of an identity crisis. It was simply not a theological question for the Palestinians at that time yet.

In the 1950s and the 1960s, shortly after the establishment of the State of Israel, there really wasn't a specific Palestinian identity as seen internationally. Arab residents of the land obviously considered themselves Palestinians, but the world saw them as part of the greater Arab world, which we could call pan-Arab.

Within this pan-Arab identity, Palestinians saw themselves as much Palestinian as they did Arab. This explains why, in 1948, the struggle

Chapter 9

against the fledgling Israeli state was seen as a struggle to reclaim Arab lands that Israel had taken.

The issue was viewed in broader geographic terms, as an Arab issue that involved Arabs from all countries in the region. Thus, at the time, the common thread that brought Palestinian Christians together was their place and participation within the larger Arab identity and community.

Not only did Palestinian Christians participate in this pan-Arab identity, but they were also leaders within it. It was the Palestinian Christians who often studied in the West who introduced some Western ideas into the pan-Arab national movement and later the Palestinian national movement.

Things began to change after 1967 when there was a push to separate the Arab and Palestinian identities. Palestinians felt that it wasn't enough for them to simply be part of the Arab world. They wanted their own place.

This happened, in part, because Israel kept winning wars against Arabs and because the pan-Arab world began making treaties with Israel that left out the Palestinians and kept them in limbo. Palestinians were angered and began to believe they couldn't trust anyone—not Israel, not the West, and no other Arab nations as well.

Christians in Palestine, thus, began to rethink their belonging and feel as part of a Palestinian identity. As such, they felt the need to be active in the struggle for the liberation of Palestine. At the time, to be identified as a Palestinian simply meant you had to be active in the struggle for an independent Palestinian state. Many of the Christians were in key (though not top) positions in the movements.

Historically, Christian-Muslim relations in Palestine and Israel have been very strong. They have been (and are) much better than in other

The Christian Arab Theology

Arab nations, such as in Syria, Iraq, Egypt, or Lebanon. One reason for this is that Christians and Muslims have been fighting together in a common struggle. The struggle has helped bridge their differences. That said, a quiet tension still exists between them in both the West Bank and in Israel.

Being a Christian minority inside a Muslim or Jewish society is difficult. I have already described many of these tensions in previous chapters. But in the end, we must continually look for ways to be part of the Palestinian identity without compromising our Christian faith.

Over time, Muslim religious thinking began to take a more predominant position within the collective Palestinian conscience. This had not been present in the pan-Arab struggle against Israel, and the change created problems for the Christians. The shift gradually pushed Christians down the ladder in terms of influence and leadership.

In the 1970s, religious Islam became much stronger and kept growing through the 1990s. This gave rise to Islamic movements within Palestinian society, and groups like Hamas (the Islamic Resistance Movement) sprang up. (As an interesting aside, the religious turn in Palestinian society mirrored Israeli society: Israelis had become more religious and nationalistic in the period, too.)

What this shift meant practically was that Palestinian Christians had to be perceived as participating in their national identity by discussing the conflict in more Islamic terms. Naturally, this created problems. Palestinian Christians needed a new way to express their identity and participate in the struggle. They needed language and understanding that reflected both their national aspirations and their Christian faith.

One complicating factor in this period was that most local churches did not represent their communities. This was because, until the late

1970s, almost all pastors and priests in Israel and Palestine were foreigners. They had been sent to the Holyland from other countries—not to serve the local congregations only but the pilgrims visiting from their home denominations. This reality caused Palestinians to feel that they needed to cater to the interests of international clergy, even if they did not say so out loud.

Things slowly began to change in this respect as local Palestinian Christians were ordained and commissioned to become heads of churches in Jerusalem and represent local Christian communities in the early 1980s. This was when local Christian leaders, for one example is His Beatitude Michel Sabbah who was the first non-Italian to hold the position as the Latin Patriarch of Jerusalem from 1987-2008 in more than five centuries, who began making statements about the conflict between Israelis and Palestinians.

Building on this, the event—or series of events—that really catalyzed a change in Palestinian Christian identity was the First Intifada (1987-1993). Tensions rose between Palestinians and Israelis to explosive levels. Additionally, Palestinian national consciousness further turned to a Muslim identity that looked suspiciously at Christians, especially if they perceived them as not sufficiently active in the resistance.

At the time, global media outlets began covering the conflict, sending news media and journalists to cover ongoing developments. And since Christians could speak western languages due to their high education levels and because so many had western connections, Christians were suddenly thrust into the spotlight.

European news channels would come to Bethlehem, for example, and Palestinian Christians were given airtime to speak about the Intifada. Christians became the spokesmen, and the Western world, for the first time, really listened.

The Christian Arab Theology

The platform and attention helped spark a revolution in Palestinian Christian thought. We did not need to cater to the interests of international clergy or western ways of thinking to gain acceptance. We realized we had our own unique culture and history. Instead of trying to be something we were not, we needed to be who we were—whom God created us to be in his divine plan. God had placed us here for a purpose.

Palestinian Christians began to read the Bible from this new position, confident in our own perspective and experience. And for us, we quickly observed that the Bible was about justice, a justice that helps the poor find salvation. Salvation was not only for the end of days or going to heaven when you die—yes, that is part of it—but salvation could be experienced right now.

This new, more active engagement with scripture began changing the way we thought about and understood our political reality. We came to believe you should not read the Bible in a way that gives legitimacy to an unjust, apartheid political system. That cannot be the right way to read scripture. The Bible is a book of justice. That is the background for Palestinian Christian Theology and what caused its emergence.

Chapter 9

The Holy Cross be My Light

Addressing the Core Questions

Let's be clear: We are a people that God has created with a unique purpose and identity. Through Jesus and his work of salvation, we are included in the multitudes of those whom God loves and blesses. We are no greater or less than any other people. We are called to love God with our whole heart, mind, and strength. We are called to live as salt and light to our neighbors, whether those neighbors be Muslims or Jews or anyone else.

Let me put it this way, the main questions our theology addresses are:

Question One: How should we read and understand the Bible?

Question Two: How should we understand the divine election and promises about the land?

Question Three: How should we understand the Israeli-Palestinian conflict?

We affirm, for example, that in the Old Testament, Israel was God's chosen people and that He gave them the land. But does that mean they have the right to take the land by force 3,000 years later? That question and others like it need thoughtful, biblically informed answers. We cannot treat them lightly.

An important point here: we believe these questions are not only for us as Palestinian Christians, but they are also for the global church. As such, Palestinian theology is written with the Western world in mind. This is done because Westerners could, in fact, do something about the conflict in the Holyland. They have influence and leverage.

This way of speaking challenges people's thinking and makes it apparent that apartheid governments and imperialism are wrong. We want people to act justly while also being careful not to make the issue about political theology. This means that although we aim to conserve our own identity, we still aim to be part of the Western churches. We are reaching out to them. We want to change the Western point of view about the conflict. Our future literally depends on it.

Now the hard part: How do we answer these three questions?

First, how do we read and understand the Bible?

We the Christians of the Holyland believe the Bible is the absolute Word of God. It is the story and history of salvation. That means the whole book is the Word of God—Old and New Testament—from Genesis 1 to Revelation 21. We cannot discard any part of it. We cannot stop reading or ignore the parts we do not like. We must read and believe all of it.

Beginning from the creation of the world to the fall of Adam, from God's covenant with Abraham and the Jewish people to the Exodus and return to the promised land, from the Babylonian exile to the return, from Jesus' life, death, and resurrection to John's final revelation—including all the details and stories between these great events—God has revealed his plan for salvation.

The Bible is the story of how we can know God and experience eternal life with him. One way we like to think of it is that when we read the Bible, we discover our own story. We find ourselves falling and then coming to God's salvation. As Adam sinned, fell, and found a way back to God, so we have fallen and have found our way back to God through Jesus.

An important point to make here is that God's revelation to humanity was progressive. This means the truth concerning God and the message of salvation were not communicated all at once. God revealed Himself over the course of the history of humankind, using the customs and cultures of humanity to unveil His gradual revelation to us. As such, a level of knowledge and understanding of God's Word corresponds to each stage of the history of the people of God.

Humanity had to go through many changes before it could cast off its polytheism and accept the one true God. It took time for the idea of monotheism to spread before humanity was able to understand the idea of a universal God and not just a particular God but one God for all. But what is the highest level of morality that humanity could achieve?

When God revealed Himself to Abraham, for example, the level and moral state of humanity were low. The pagan, polytheistic humanity of Abraham's day could not understand the idea of a universal God and the idea of a single God. So, when God first revealed Himself to humanity, He did it as the God of a particular people—Abraham's descendants, the Jews. God gave the Holyland to the Jews so that they could be a light to the world concerning this one, single, and all-powerful God.

Why is this concept important? It is because it relates to the way we understand divine election. God needed to choose the people of Israel because that was the only way, at the time, for humanity to understand His divinity. God needed to promise Israel the land because He needed them to build Him a temple. Back then, the concept of divinity, centered around a place. All the gods of the nations lived in and were worshiped in different places.

God, thus, needed a single place in the world where people could look and see what He was like. God had to demonstrate that He was greater than the gods of all the other nations, and that those other gods were not even gods in comparison. Before other nations could come to believe in the one true God, they had to understand through the example of a single nation.

Chapter 9

But we also know from the Old Testament that God's intentions for salvation were never for the people of Israel exclusively. God offered hints that His intentions for salvation included all nations. Take (Psalm 67) that begins, "May God be gracious to us and bless us and make his face shine on us—so that your ways may be known on earth, your salvation among all nations." This is one example among many. This is an early indicators of the fact that God intended to make salvation possible for all humanity from any tribe, tongue, family, or nation.

Progressing through Biblical history, the climax of salvation history is found in Jesus. His life and teaching, his death and resurrection made salvation possible for anyone who believes. Jesus is the way, the truth, and the life, our way back to God in a restored relationship. Jesus is salvation. As such, Jesus is the key to understanding the Bible. Every page must be read through the lens of his saving work on the cross. And he made salvation possible for all people on earth.

God never changes, but the way He deals with humanity does. He first chose Abraham to make a nation and worked through the prophets and the Jewish people. Today, He works through His Son and establishes the church through His Holy Spirit.

I think of this like a doctor. Since we are humans and fragile, we get sick and need to visit the doctor occasionally. But you would never expect your doctor to give you the same treatment for a broken bone as you would for the flu. For a broken leg, your doctor may ask for an x-ray to see how to set it correctly, to see exactly where the fracture is and how to go about setting it straight. But they would not call for an x-ray to diagnose the flu when they could use a stethoscope to hear your breathing or use a light to inspect the back of your throat.

Doctors prescribe different treatments according to symptoms and the need. Neither can we expect God to deal with humanity's changing issues in the same way as He once did. The methods and treatment might change, but the doctor—God—does not change. God's purpose remains the same, to bring healing to the part that is broken.

Hopefully, this helps you understand a little bit more how we, the Palestinian Christians, read the Bible and why. We hold the stick from the middle because if we hold it from either side, it will start hurting others and even sometimes can hurt us too. Now, after Christ, we understand God's salvation plan much better. We understand that it is no longer that important to have one specific central place, such as a temple, to worship God.

This foundation leads to the second key question: How should we understand divine election and God's promises about the land?

What if you happen to be a Palestinian Arab Christian, and you find that you are identified in the minds of the Israeli Jews with the ancient Canaanites and all the other tribes which Joshua defeated in the thirteenth century before Christ.

How are you likely to think about the book that seems to give the Jews a divine right to take away your land in the 20th century? Since they believed that they were the chosen people who enjoyed a special relationship with God, they acted on their history in such a way as to justify their ideas about their special status and their superiority over other people.

Christian Zionists cause additional problems for Christians as well as in the Middle East when they are very vocal and expressive in their unconditional support for Israel to reestablish a Jewish homeland as marked out in the biblical verses.

To do so, Israel would have to occupy not only the West Bank and Gaza but also Jordan, pieces of Egypt, Iraq, Syria, and Lebanon.

Chapter 9

Christian Zionists confuse today's State of Israel with biblical Israel, the former being mostly a secular entity that rejects Jesus.

This means Israel is still God's chosen people, they still have a very significant and unique covenant with God, but it does not mean all the implications of the covenant and the promises are relevant to our time. This is why we cannot speak about the promises and the elections of the Bible as something that should have political implications in our time.

I will add a few more thoughts here. Why did God choose a people? It is not because the chosen people were more excellent than others or because of their merits. God's choice rather reflected His wisdom and love. Deuteronomy 9:5 declares, "It is not because of your righteousness or the uprightness of your heart that you go in to possess their land, but because of the wickedness of these nations that the Lord your God drives them out from before you, and that he may fulfill the word which the Lord swore to your fathers, to Abraham, Isaac, and Jacob."

That God chooses a person, and grants him a particular grace, does not mean that He rejects other people or deprives them of His grace. God's grace is given to many, and each person receives His grace. Jesus declared that there are many dwelling places in His Father's house.

The land belongs to those whom God has allowed to enter it as His guests—as long as they are not unworthy of dwelling in it. Because of the wickedness of those nations, the Lord drove them out before Israel.

So too, the chosen people were required to remain worthy of the land by observing God's law. They had to remain faithful to the grace they had received. Once they had occupied the land, they had to continue to merit it in order to preserve it, or else the land would vomit them out.

Don't think that God chose Israel because they were better than someone else. It was simply part of His design for His salvation plan. In the end, He will choose everybody and wants all the nations to be saved. He will give His grace to all people and give them a mission in His salvation plan. We are all one; all humanity is made in God's image, so He loves all of His creation.

There is no difference between those who are Jews and others who have been chosen by God in a different way. When we talk about God choosing a people or choosing a person, we mean God is giving him the responsibility to fulfill a mission to complete. In God's grace, there is no race. The land does not belong to any one specific anymore. It belongs only to God.

Simply because Israel was promised the land once historically does not mean they should have unchallenged ownership of the land today. If Israel wanted to stay in the land, they had to follow and observe God's law. They need to remain faithful and worthy. They need to respect the other people living in the land, fighting for the human rights of all people and all other religions in the land.

With that in mind, what about the current conflict in the Holyland? This is the third question. The essential question asked by the Palestinian Christians and by every believer in the Bible is this: does the Bible, as the Word of God, give the right to the Jewish people today to appropriate the land for themselves and, in doing so, dispossess the Palestinian people?

On the one hand, God promised the land to Abraham and his descendants. But on the other, for centuries, this land has belonged to another people, the Palestinian people. Even in Biblical times, the land was inhabited by other peoples. Take the Canaanites, for example, they coexisted with the Jewish people.

The land was also the location of the most important events of Christianity. It is also Christianity's Holyland, par excellence. We could say the same thing about Islam, the land is holy for Muslims, too. Three peoples, therefore, have political rights in the same land, and three religions also have religious rights here. The three religions are the descendants, physical or spiritual, of Abraham, the person to whom God had promised the land.

Then, to whom does the land belong? Today, if one of the three religions were to claim, in the name of their religion, a political right to the land, then the two other parties would have the right to lay the same claim on the same ground. The Palestinian Christian theologians are looking at this from a biblical perspective. They are saying that we cannot speak about the political situation with religious claims since all three religions have equal claims.

Instead, Palestinian Christian theologians are approaching the issue from a different perspective. They argue that we should not use the Bible to oppress others. We shouldn't abuse the biblical text in order to lay claim to power. At the same time, we have the right to read the biblical text as it applies to us. Justice is the central message, and this is how many Western societies understand human rights and divine justice also.

It is no wonder that most of the statements about election in the Old Testament date from the time of Israel's exile. It is a promise to those, above all, who see themselves as unworthy, weak, and powerless. It is to them that God promises election. This principle is true today for the humble and meek Christians that are so little regarded.

The Christian Arab Theology

If the Jews, who were driven out of Europe and suffered the Holocaust, saw a fulfillment of the Old Testament promises about land in their immigration to Palestine, then this should be honored and respected as a testimony and expression of their faith. But today, one must be clear about what it means to persist in talking about the promise of land and its fulfillment in the State of Israel.

In Israel today, public reference to the promise of land is used by radical fundamentalist groups to justify continued occupation of the West Bank and Gaza. We know this is a hot topic that Palestinian theologians are struggling to explain to the international Christian world.

It is important to understand that the Palestinian Christian theologians are not saying that we should dismiss the covenant with Israel, and neither are they saying it has been canceled or replaced. We are not talking of a replacement or a liberation theology but of a fulfillment theology. ***It is this fulfillment theology that connects the old and the new covenants.*** We are not talking about two different covenants, but that the covenant was fulfilled.

Before I move on, I want to acknowledge that in my brief answers to these questions, I have likely raised more questions than answers for you. I'm certain I have left out different aspects of this discussion that might be helpful. If you'd like to delve deeper into this topic, I suggest you read some books on Palestinian Christian Theology directly. You can find a few helpful references in the Bibliography.

Chapter 9

The Theology of the Land

When Abraham—the patriarch of Jews, Christians, and Muslims—first came to the land, he continued his semi-nomadic way of life. Moved to the hill country, pitching his tents between Shechem, Bethel, and Hebron. He did not assume God's promise about the land gave him the right to steal it from its then-owners. He was not interested in accepting land as a gift either. He insisted on legally buying a cave at full value.

If the land was a gift, which carried with it an obligation to obey the law of God, then it followed naturally that when this obligation was not honored, the gift would lose its purpose and no longer serve in the way it once did. The children of Israel were not to assume that they could live in the land forever, regardless of the way they lived. While the promise and gift of the land were unconditional, their continued possession of the land depended on their loyalty and obedience to God.

Abraham had been promised that he would be the ancestor of a great nation and that through his descendants, all peoples on earth would be blessed. Later, through Jesus, God's plan for the Jewish people entered a new phase, one which included people of all races, lands, and cultures within the loving purposes of God. Jesus spelled out His understanding of who the true people of God were. Jesus as well, extended God's blessing to anyone who is poor in spirit, anyone who hungers and thirsts for righteousness.

One way to think about it is that Joshua described the gradual conquest of the land beginning from Jericho. The book of Acts described the gradual spread of the Christian church beginning from Jerusalem. Joshua and the tribes were to possess their allotted inheritance by killing its inhabitants with the edge of the sword.

In Acts, Paul speaks of the Word of God as the weapon by which Christians are to occupy their inheritance. The book of Acts describes how the Gospel was first preached in Jerusalem, in Samaria, and then in Caesarea to the first Gentile. And then, from Antioch, Paul took the message into Asia Minor, to Greece, and finally to Rome. Interestingly, the story in Acts of Ananias and Sapphira and their deception over the sale of their land is an exact parallel to the story of Joshua and Achkan, whose theft and treachery held up the advance of the whole army in (Joshua 7).

If Luke and the early Christian church thought in terms of conquest, they were thinking in terms of the whole world, not a small portion of it. And importantly: the only sword that would be used for this conquest was the Word of God, which would enable those who believed it to possess the inheritance that God had promised them.

The spiritual Israel embraces all who have taken up their cross to follow in the footsteps of the crucified Messiah. Christians have no territorial center, no physical land or place that is the focus of faith and worship because Jesus Christ has taken on the full theological and spiritual significance that the land, city, and temple had held for Israel. It is now open to the people of all nations.

Most, if not all, Christians believe that the temple and its sacrifices have been fulfilled once and for all in Jesus. This means we no longer expect to see a pure literal fulfillment. Jesus is our fulfillment. It is a progressive revelation climaxing in the person of Jesus.

God made a covenant with Abraham, promising him that his descendants would inherit the land between Egypt and the Euphrates River. Thus, the Jews believe they have a divine right to the land for all time. Let me use an Old Testament story that illustrates my point.

CHAPTER 9

King Ahab, one of the worst kings of Israel, married Jezebel, a most wicked woman who introduced the worship of Baal. No doubt, Ahab had many good reasons for trying to obtain possession of the vineyard belonging to Naboth, which adjoined his own property. His first attempt to acquire the vineyard was perfectly fair and above board: "So Ahab spoke to Naboth, 'Give me your vineyard, that I may have it for a vegetable garden, because it is near, next to my house, and for it, I will give you a vineyard better than it. Or, if it seems good to you, I will give you its' worth in money" (1 Kings 21:2).

However, the vineyard was worth more to Naboth than its cash value because it was part of his family's inheritance, and he refused to sell it: "But Naboth said to Ahab, The lord forbid that I should give you the inheritance of my fathers" (1 Kings 21:3). Urged on by Jezebel, his wife, Ahab then restored to deceit and finally to violence. The sequel to the story indicates the seriousness of Ahab's crimes in the eyes of God.

When reduced to its essence, it embodies the tragedy of Palestine as well as the suppression of the rights of the individual. But it is more a story of tragedy since, at its heart, there stands the God of justice, who governs history, who has a long memory, and who will not allow injustice to go unchecked forever.

In this day, God is dealing with His people through a spiritual method —by His Holy Spirit. This change, however, had to be gradual, as has already been explained. So now, all the privileges and titles that were related to the Jewish people in the Old Testament, like a chosen people, a royal priesthood, a holy nation, and a people belonging to God, are now applied to people of all nationalities who believe in Jesus Christ.

Jesus the Messiah, who lived, died, and was raised from the dead, has opened the Kingdom of God to people of all races, making all who follow Him into one people. Jesus told us that He was the way, not the law, not the Torah, and not anything else. Jesus gave us a new vision, one of being more open and inclusive. He invited all to follow Him. He was able to push past the boundaries that Judaism had put around itself and see a whole world out there that should not be ignored.

Jesus was born under occupation and lived all His life under occupation. During his early years, His family became refugees and had to flee to Egypt. The Jewishness of Jesus is a source of hope for me. He came from Jewish roots but asked for peace, justice, and equality for all humans. Personally, I also emphasize his Jewish identity to understand His ministry more and to become a better disciple of Him.

Israel is here now, and there's likely nothing that will change it. There were and are injustices, people losing more and more land, and we should speak about these things. But I don't want to connect this Israel to the Bible. Yes, it's here to stay, but not because of the Bible.

Christian Zionism is a modern theological and political movement that embraces the most extreme ideological positions of Zionism. This inevitably leads to unending cycles of violence that undermine the security of all people of the Middle East and the rest of the world.

We call upon Christians in churches on every continent to pray for the Palestinian and Israeli people, both of whom are suffering and are victims of occupation and militarism. Discriminative actions have turned Palestine into impoverished ghettos surrounded by exclusive Israeli settlements.

The establishment of these illegal settlements and the construction of the separation wall, which amounted to more confiscated Palestinian land, has undermined the viability of peace and security in the entire region. The west passed from antisemitism to Philo-Semitism—blind love for the modern State of Israel not based on truth but based on emotions only.

Because the Jews believe they were chosen by God, they have developed prejudice, thinking they are a better nation than any other nation in the world. This feeling of entitlement has created many problems in the Middle East that we have today.

But were God's promises to ancient Israel unconditional? The Old Testament is full of evidence that those promises were conditional on the faithfulness and obedience of the people of Israel to God. Yet God still fulfilled His purpose through them and blessed all the nations of the world through Abraham's seed, that is, through Jesus Christ.

We affirm that Israelis and Palestinians can live together in peace and security. We call upon all people to reject the narrow worldview of Christian Zionism and other ideologies that privilege one people above others. God demands that justice be done, and no enduring peace, security, or reconciliation is possible without the foundation of justice. The struggle for justice must be pursued diligently and persistently, but also nonviolently.

This is where we take our stand. We stand for justice. Justice alone guarantees peace that will lead to reconciliation with a life of security and prosperity for all the peoples of our land. In the eyes of God, yes, we are equal, but in the eyes of the Jewish and Muslim people, Christians are not equal.

Moreover, when the Muslim world sees how many millions of so-called Bible-believing Christians in the West support the policies of Israel, they reject the Christian message out of hand and are unwilling to listen to any Christian who wants to speak about the love of God in

Jesus. Religious observance is meaningless in an unjust society. Zion will be redeemed through righteousness and not by any other means.

In summary, God's plan and love are for all humanity to be united in Christ. Christianity is no longer limited to a single ethnic group. All who believe and accept the work of Christ on the cross become part of the family of God and inherit the promises of the new covenant fulfilled in Christ.

It is a narrow path and hard to follow, but at the end of the path is healing. This is where all the parts of the hidden bridge are being united together, and the bridge is now strong enough for all to cross over it. At the heavenly banquet table, there is neither male nor female, rich nor poor, Jew nor Arab. We will all rejoice His presence, which is the most essential of all.

Chapter 10

The Parable of the Good Samaritan

Here at the end of the book, I would like to set aside the complex and sensitive topics of the previous chapter and offer a few reflections on the parable of the Good Samaritan. This parable, more than any other, influences the way I think about—and practically apply—the material covered in the previous chapter. In the end, what matters most is stooping down, getting yourself dirty, and helping the needy person. That is the hidden bridge revealed.

Chapter 10

Part of the ancient Jerusalem- Jericho Road

The Parable of the Good Samaritan

Background of the Parable

Like any other parable, we need to understand the cultural background first to grasp the significance of Jesus' most famous parable, found only in (Luke 10). Notice that Jesus was in Jericho when He began the parable. But after He finished, we find him in Bethany, just outside of Jerusalem. The disciples may have been walking alongside Jesus on that very road when he told them this story.

Why is the road between Jerusalem and Jericho so dangerous?

First, the zealots had a command post in Wadi-Qelt, a place near the road. The Zealots typically lived in caves near this road, staying away from the Romans. And their main source of income was robbing pilgrims who walked along the way. That means no one listening to Jesus tell this parable would have been surprised that a man traveling alone on the road from Jericho to Jerusalem was robbed.

Second, in this road, is one of the few places in the country where archeologists have (thus far) found bones showing where someone died of leprosy. In Jesus' day, lepers were not allowed to live in cities or villages. They had to make their home in the wilderness and often formed bands and groups to help out one another. And how do you suppose they made their living? Just like the Zealots—by robbing people passing by. The road between Jericho and Jerusalem was scary to pass.

In addition, of course, it was not only the zealots and lepers who made the road dangerous. The road was steep and dry (as it is today). Most of the year, the road was hot, and there were many curves. Traveling it by night in the dark would be the height of folly. These dangers made it such that most people made the long trip up the hill in a single day and in large groups so they could have safety in numbers.

Chapter 10

This was not the road where someone would be included to stop to help a single person on lying in the ditch. Complicating things further —that person laying there could be playing a trick, trying to get you to stop, so they could rob you. My guess is that the disciples would have rather heard this parable on any road except this road. It's more comfortable to think about the story abstractly, not while you're walking along the road.

The Wounded Man

In light of this, listen to how the parable begins: A man went from Jerusalem to Jericho. One man!

Remember: a parable is a story that is meant to shock you. They often begin with something that contradicts common sense. The teller wants to grab your attention. One man—alone—traveling from Jericho to Jerusalem. That's shocking. People always traveled on that road in groups. Typically, groups consisted of several men, followed by a group of women and children, who were then followed by another group of men.

Given that the man was traveling alone, it's no surprise to learn that he fell in among thieves and was robbed. More than that: he was beaten, stripped of his clothes, and left unconscious. These details are important to understand the story.

Back then, the way people could tell a person's background was by their clothing and their accent. But this man was stripped of his clothes and unconscious. No one could tell if he was a Jew, or a Gentile. They had no way to identify his social standing or nationality. He was the perfect stranger. A big risk to approach.

According to the cultural norms of the day, higher-class individuals were not expected to help those of a lower social situation.

The Parable of the Good Samaritan

Occasionally, however, lower-class individuals might help a higher-class person to improve their own social standing. But since there was no way to identify the unconscious man's social standing from his clothing, no one would have been motivated to help him, even if their motives were self-focused.

The man's accent would have also tipped people off about his status. Then as now, different ethnic groups in the Middle East are identified by the way they use their language by their accent. In the first century, Jewish scholars could speak Hebrew, while peasants spoke Aramaic. Along the Sea of Galilee, Syriac was in use. The Greek cities naturally conversed in Greek, and tribesmen in the south spoke Arabic. Government officials would have known formal Greek. Which one of these groups did the man belong to? No one could tell.

Accent and dress would have been the clues needed to distinguish the man's identity and status. The only thing that could be said about this man as that he was a stranger. As you start to see the brilliant way Jesus crafted the story.

That said, we do know one other thing about him. He was a fool. He traveled all alone on a dangerous road that everyone knew was dangerous. But there's more: most robbers have a certain etiquette that they follow. If you give them what they want, they normally don't beat you up. But if you resist, then they are going to beat you.

This was true of robbers in the Middle East in Jesus' day. They were known to beat their victims—only—if they resisted. We can assume, therefore, that this guy made the mistake of resisting and consequently suffered a severe beating. He was left naked and unconscious on the side of the road.

Chapter 10

The Priest and the Levite

Let's turn our attention to the men who passed him by without helping. One was a priest and the other was a Levite. They were probably heading home after their temple service and most likely traveling with a group, perhaps one of fellow priests or Levites.

At the time, the temple in Jerusalem was served by three classes of people. Priests comprised the first, the second was the Levites, and the third were laymen who helped with various aspects of the life of the temple. All three are important to the story.

The priest was on his way down the mountain from Jerusalem to Jericho. Many priests in the first century lived in Jericho, especially in the winter. They would go up to Jerusalem for a two-week assignment and then return to their homes in Jericho. This priest would have fit easily into such a pattern. Priests at the time were a hereditary guild and were known to be wealthy. Toward the close of the second temple period, the priesthood constituted the prestigious and elite class in the Jewish society.

At first glance, the wounded, unconscious man could have looked dead. If so, the priest would become ceremonially unclean if he approached him. The same ban would apply to his family and servants, those traveling with him. Then if he were to become unclean, he would need to undergo a week-long process of ceremonial purification. It would take some time to arrange such things. He would have spent a week going through ritual immersion baths and having ashes from the red heifer dumped over himself. It was a miserable process. Much easier to walk by.

Also, if he was coming the other way, up the hill, from Jericho to Jerusalem, taking the seven required days to purify him would mean missing part of his service. This would be more costly for the priest.

The Parable of the Good Samaritan

Also, the decision would be fraught with danger. If he became defiled and tried to serve at the altar in a state of uncleanness, young men could take him outside the temple court and break open his head with clubs. Even the risk of being accused would be frightening. He probably reasoned to himself that his ministry of interceding for Israel was more important than one man. Helping that man would be possible but inconvenient, a distraction from something more important.

What's more, the victim along the road might have been Egyptian, Greek, Syrian or Phoenician. In this case, the priest was not responsible under the law to do anything. The priest would not have had an easy time determining his obligation since the man was unclothed and unconscious.

These factors combined—purity, defilement, inconvenience, and legal obligation—mean the priest likely decided that the chance of becoming ceremonially unclean was simply too risky. Easier to walk away. Jesus included a person with real and important religious justifications for not stopping.

This makes me wonder: How often do the rules, regulations, and laws established to facilitate our work or simplify our decision-making become aims in themselves rather than means to accomplishing our aims? We live in a world dominated by self-interest, superiority, pride, power, authority, and sovereignty.

Let's now turn to the Levite coming down the same road and seeing the same wounded man. He appears to have been more curious than the priest and actually approached the unconscious man. But he did not help him either.

The Levite would have been a servant in the temple, an assistant to the priests. He would have had the same ceremonial obligations of purity to consider. He would also have the complicated dynamic of inadvertently undermining his overseer.

Could the Levite ride into Jericho with a wounded man whom the priest, in obedience to his understanding of the law, had opted to ignore? Such an act would be an insult to the priest! The flip side to this dynamic is that since the priest had set a precedent of not stopping, the Levite could pass by with an easy conscience.

Both these men, the priest and Levite, may also have hoped the next person who came down the road could help, someone who was less busy, better suited, or better equipped with the right resources. Both the priest and the Levite were likely seeking, perhaps unawares, to be righteous in their own eyes and their own circles rather than in the eyes of God! Thus, they thought to silence their conscience, justifying their decisions by sticking to the rules and regulations of their religious obligations.

Those listening to the parable, those who heard Jesus talk about a priest and then a Levite would have naturally assumed the third man coming down the road was a Jewish layman, someone who worked in the temple as a volunteer or non-professional. But that's not what happened. The story took an unexpected twist and exploded in the face of Jesus' listeners.

The Good Samaritan

Jesus brought an unexpected character into the story, a Samaritan. The Samaritan passerby saw the man lying naked and unconscious on the side of the road, stopped and stooped to help immediately. What's so unexpected about this? The Samaritans were the Jew's enemies.

The history of hatred between Jews and Samaritans went all the way back to when the king of Assyria brought foreign tribes into Samaria.

These people married the local Jews and had children. These offspring were half-bred Jews caught between the traditions of Judaism and Assyrians. The Jews began to look down upon them as ethnically compromised religious heretics.

If Jesus had made the wounded man a Jew, the story would have been more acceptable to His audience. Easier to swallow. Jesus could have also told a story about a Jewish person who helped a Samaritan that had been wounded. The Jewish audience would have found it within themselves to praise a good Jew, even though the needy person was a Samaritan. That's pure virtue.

It is, however, a different matter to tell a story about a good Samaritan who helps a wounded Jew in the Judean wilderness of Judah, especially after the Jewish priest and Levite fail to turn aside to assist the unconscious stranger.

Why did Jesus make the Samaritan into a good guy? It wasn't because Samaritans were always good in history. They had their faults. Jesus took what the Jews despised most and made them deal with it.

Before I discuss this more, I need to remind you that Jesus shared this parable in answer to a very specific question from a very specific person. First the question: "Who is my neighbor?" Jesus and his listeners both would have known Leviticus 19:18, where it says, "You shall not take vengeance nor bear any grudge against the children of your people, but you shall *love your neighbor as yourself*: I am the Lord." The Jewish people understood the verse in Leviticus to mean members of your own nation.

The Torah says that we should love our neighbor as ourselves. The Jews understood a neighbor to be someone from their own community, a friend, or another fellow Jew. The word "neighbor" could mean a friend. So, loving your friend as yourself makes sense.

Chapter 10

And that means the priest and Levite acted in a way that they thought was appropriate according to the Torah. This person was not their friend, so they did not need to act like a friend. They were under no obligation.

But Jesus' was challenging the interpretation of who a neighbor is according to the Torah. He redefined who your neighbor could and should be. In Jesus' day, Samaritans were enemies of the Jews. He wanted to include people not from your nation, even those considered enemies. This is where Jesus shocked His listeners. He made it clear that a neighbor could be anyone, including an enemy.

Let's now think about the person asking the question. He was an expert in the law, a lawyer. Jesus knew the man was trying to justify himself that he *had* kept the law. But Jesus explained that to keep the law, the man would also love his enemy.

Notice how the one who asked could not even bring himself to say the word Samaritan after Jesus told the story. His prejudice ran so deep that the name was unspeakable. He only referred to him indirectly as 'the one who showed mercy.' In a way, that is still a good way to refer to the Samaritan. Mercy does not depend on family bonds, tribal ties, nationality, religion, or class—it only sees another human being.

It did not matter what the injured, unconscious person's social standing was, what language he spoke, or his ethnic origin. The important thing was being a neighbor to whomever you encountered along the way. But Jesus did this to make us realize that mercy and compassion come above all other considerations in our dealings with every human being, regardless of identity, social class, or any other factor. Jesus was saying that you can be a Priest, Levite, an Israelite, or even a Samaritan; you should love your neighbor.

The Parable of the Good Samaritan

This story would be equally shocking today if it was a Palestinian helping an injured Jew— "The Good Palestinian." It is simply unexpected and culturally unacceptable to tell a Jewish audience a story where a Palestinian is the hero.

Or, putting the story into an American historical context, suppose a Native American found a cowboy with two arrows in his back laying on the side of the road— "The Good Native American"—then dismounted his horse, placed the cowboy on his horse, and took him to Dodge City for medical treatment. After checking into a room over the saloon, the man would then spend the night taking care of the cowboy. How would the people of Dodge City react to such a scene? Most people know the Native American man would likely be killed.

Moreover, the good Samaritan in the story is a type of Jesus. First-aid was administered, and his wounds were bound and disinfected. In the first century, a wound was bound first, and then wine and oil were poured on the bandages to soak through to the wound. The Samaritan would have used all his available resources, oil, wine, a cloth wrapping, riding animal, time, energy, and money, to care for the wounded man. Put in this context, we can see that the Samaritan paid a high price to assist the stranger, likely even risking his life to take him to a Jewish inn within Jewish territory.

The listener to the story would naturally expect the Samaritan to take the wounded man down to Jericho and then leave him at the edge of the city and disappear. A Samaritan would not be safe in a Jewish town with a wounded Jew over the back of his riding animal. His actions could easily be misunderstood, and he could have been blamed for the Jew's condition.

Jesus often used non-Jews in order to shame His own people and to point out that these people who were not part of the Jewish covenant were more faithful than they. I believe Jesus was pushing the point that humans are made in the image of God, so each and every one of them is important—contrary to typical religious Jewish thought.

As Christ's followers, we don't only help other Christians. Jesus taught us to help everyone. Who is our neighbor? Who is it that we are to love as ourselves? The answer is everyone—even our enemies.

One of the things in the second and third centuries that impressed the Romans and Roman philosophers was Christians who helped anyone, not only other Christians. The influence of this parable on Christian values was profound.

I need to mention something else, though, too: It is always easier to help an innocent victim of circumstances or another person's actions. It's much harder to help someone who is in trouble because of their own stupidity.

I find it interesting that Jesus told the parable about someone who got in trouble because of their own stupidity. This means we should not withhold help from people who are in trouble because of their own foolishness. We are to help anyone in need. Period. Your neighbor is anyone in need, and it does not matter what their religion is, color is, or what social background they may have.

This parable shows the love of God. When we were in trouble because of our foolishness and sin, God sent Jesus to save us. This is His work. He went so far beyond for us, more than what we deserved. We are the wounded man on the side of the road. The wounded man is us. Jesus did more for us than expose himself to ritual impurity for a week. He paid the penalty for our sins.

It is all paid by the blood of Jesus, and we can come to Him and receive salvation. He is our Good Samaritan. Our sins mean we are nearly dead, unconscious. But all we must do is allow Jesus to come to us. So, I say to you, let the Good Samaritan poor oil and wine into your spiritual wounds. Oil and wine are symbols of the Holy Spirit. To inherit eternal life, all we must do is consistently practice the unqualified love of God and transmit this love that we receive to our neighbors.

Whatever you think about the conflict politically or theologically—whether or not you agree with my account of Palestinian Christian Theology—we can all become more like the Good Samaritan. We find the hidden bridge and start to walk it when we bend over and help someone in need. That is the hidden bridge revealed.

Epilogue

How Can You Help?

No doubt, the pages of this book have shown you that there are many differences between Middle Eastern Christians and those in the West. Language, culture, and geography separate us. But what brings us together—the most important thing—is Jesus Christ.

I meet Christian tourists and pilgrims almost every week. And from our very first interaction, I feel a kindred spirit with them. This is the Spirit of God working in us. The love of His Son unites our spirit. It transcends our many differences. For me, this is the strongest evidence that our God is one and true.

I am always encouraged, especially when guiding Christian groups because they remind me that we the local Holyland Christians are not alone, that other believers share our concerns, and that other believers are open to sharing our sufferings and joys. One question these people ask me regularly is: *"How can I help?"* This is a beautiful question, and I always love answering it.

I'd like to start with the most important thing: PRAYER. Please pray for all people of the land. That's what we, as Christians, are called to do no matter where we are from. Christians everywhere are called to prayer. We must return the land we call holy to a place of wholeness, peace, redemption, and reconciliation for all of its inhabitants. This will bring peace to the Holyland and then to the whole world. It will only happen through prayer.

Pray for Jews and Muslims—and don't just pick one of the two groups. It's better to pray for both. That will keep your heart soft toward the needs, challenges, and joys of each. A moment ago, I mentioned feeling kindred spirits with the Christian tourists and pilgrims that I meet. Sadly, I don't experience this with Jews and Muslims. Yes, we share many things, such as language and culture, and these things bring us together in some meaningful ways, but the spirit of their faith is totally different.

With Jews, I regularly sense a spirit of arrogance. For Muslims, it's the opposite. I sense inferiority. Even though we are neighbors and see each other daily, the moment we start to talk about religion, we start quarreling. I do not sense the spirit of love in them that we receive from Christ. I do not say this from a sense of superiority either, that somehow my religion makes me better than them.

No! It's the opposite. When I interact with people who do not know Jesus (whatever I perceive in their spirits), it fills me with love and compassion. It makes me want to share the love of God with them. God's love through Jesus is good news. So, pray that both Jews and Muslims would be open and receptive to the good news of Jesus.

Epilogue

Pray for us the Christians of the Holyland. Pray that we would learn from each other and not be afraid of other cultures. The church of the Holyland may be small, but we are a bridge, the hidden bridge, between both sides of the conflict. Pray that the Palestinian Christians throughout the Holyland—in Israel, Jerusalem, the West Bank, and Gaza—would be the model to promote healthy, loving Christian-Muslim and Christian-Jewish relations.

God has put us, the Christians of the Holyland, in a strategic position to reach out to our Jewish and Muslim neighbors. We know their culture and have been living with them for centuries. Pray that we would faithfully live out the calling God has placed on our lives to be that hidden bridge.

Wherever you live in the east or the west, you can designate a regular day for prayer and reflections for peace in Israel, in Palestine, and in the Middle East. You can do it by yourself, or you can gather some friends and fellow believers in your home or church. Start discussing and praying through these issues. That's a great way to get involved.

What opportunities are there beyond prayer? You can also VISIT. You can help increase community-based pilgrimages and authentic tourism to the Holyland. You can get first-hand experience getting to know the Christians of the Holyland, their hopes and fears, their challenges and contributions. Christians have always been a minority within a sea of Jews and an ocean of Islam, but we've always been and will keep on surviving.

One thing that keeps us going is seeing you. Therefore, even your smallest encouragement, as simple as visiting the land and interacting with its Christian community, is very helpful for the local church beyond what you can imagine.

Epilogue

I am grateful to The Cross Church in Wylie, TX, and specifically Mrs. Debra Tobolka for inviting me to the States for the first time many years ago. That experience helped get me started. As well as Mrs. Norvi M. Mayfield from the Mayfield foundation that has been a constant source of support and encouragement, by her empowering missions ministry. This is quickly to mention those few people and, definitely Pastor Craig Andrus from Christians Heights Assembly of God, Sonora, California as well.

It is not a secret that the Christian minority in the Middle East, in general, and in Israel, in particular, is facing crises with its identity. We are wondering where we belong in the changing tides of the times. Therefore, the church should help its members to connect with their own people in love, sincerity, and care. In this way, Christians can bring their biblical values and the teaching of the Gospel to their own people and to the overseas' church as well.

This is why your visit is important. We need you to understand this complicated issue. It is not only politics mixed with religion, but even more, it is a spiritual conflict that has lasted for a long time now. Palestinians seek justice, while Jews want security. This cycle will continue until both sides get to experience the love of God.

It is the love of God that is the most important to overwhelm our hearts first before we start accusing each other. We call upon all churches to break their silence and speak for reconciliation in the Holyland.

We need your encouragement too. Those who have visited the Holyland through Twins Tours have been an amazing encouragement and blessing to me. This has helped me, my community, and my church to keep holding on and continuing in our faith. So, one thing you can do is start strengthening the Christian presence in the Holyland, engage in mutual visits and exchanges with the churches

Epilogue

and their leaders, and resolve for an ongoing commitment to peace and justice.

With more and more of the world rejecting racism, the eyes of the Western world have turned to the Palestinian-Israeli conflict. Christian groups have risen up to fight against injustice, wanting to hear from the indigenous Christians themselves. In addition, do invite the Christians of the Holyland to your churches to speak; that is a great way to get involved and help.

Also, tourism is one other way that can contribute to the consciousness of this relationship and can strengthen our Christian identity. A tour through the country offers the perfect opportunity to gain a better understanding of this relationship and take a closer look at specific details along the tour. We, the local guides, can explain things much better than what is written in books. The words of this book are just to whet your appetite and provide you with a small taste of what you will experience.

Twins Tours & Travel Ltd. is a boutique Christian travel agency, that cannot compete with the larger Jewish or Muslim agencies. But no matter our size, we believe God can use us. Our company gives us the opportunity to be living witnesses for people throughout the Holyland and even all around the world. Me and my twin brother, Andre, see ourselves as two small hinges that can help to move and thus open doors in God's Kingdom. Join one of our tours so that you can find the needed keys to open unexpected doors in your lives.

Our specialty is biblical study tours. We focus on helping visitors better understand the connections between the Bible culture and the heritage of the people of this land. The people of the region have more or less kept these traditions throughout history. We are the heirs of the biblical culture and of the land of the Bible.

Epilogue

Many people we work with in the industry do not understand how we can continually be honest and work with integrity. Sometimes they even perceive our God-honoring business practices as threatening.

Unfortunately, there are many examples of misusing tourists by both the Jews and the Muslims, and this really breaks my heart because the tourists usually are not fully aware of what is going on around them. They find out after it is too late. But for us, integrity and honesty are issues of first importance to our Christian faith.

It breaks me when I see Western Christians blindly trusting Jewish and Muslim tour guides who mistreat and cast doubts upon the local Christian population. We Christians are honest and straightforward and can only tell the truth, not like others who just smile and try to help because they want something else from you.

Many Muslims have these wrong ideas about the West, especially the United States. They see the States as a country of war and other wrong ideas of freedom, something they often get from the TV and the internet.

Also, the Jews want to misuse their relationship with the West to benefit only themselves. It will be too late by the time you realize you have been cheated by most of the Jews that you have blindly loved. I wish you would have listened instead to the Christians who you have mistreated. We simply care for you and are more interested in your success than just for any personal benefit.

To be clear, the tourism industry will always smile and be kind because they are used to doing that. They are experts in doing it, for they know this is the fastest way to fulfill their greed and get your money.

But often, the moment you turn your back, they will start cursing you because all they care about is fulfilling their unhealthy desires. We,

EPILOGUE

however, are more interested in building up the Body of Christ and serving our fellow Christians from all over the world. So don't be misled!

I am saying that most of all the tourist companies only care about their own welfare. But we try to work with the few remaining who really care about the benefit of their customers.

It takes a few years for some tour leaders to start trusting us, but when they do, they can see the difference. We can see how both the Jews and Muslims look at us, for when they see our success, they get literally jealous and upset at us.

We always return to Christ, the foundation of our faith. Church and prayer are what matters most. God is going to restore His church, and this volcano will not remain dormant. One day it will explode again from Jerusalem to all over the world.

You are welcome to join one of our tours and see for yourself as we drive through this beautiful country and take you through a lot of the biblical places in both Israel and the west Bank where many non-Christian-based tour companies hesitate to go to. There are many more biblical insights that you'll discover that can't be all written in this book, but the few examples herein will help you taste the faithfulness of our Lord!

Epilogue

A Final Word

Let's review. I am an Israeli but not a Jew. I am a Palestinian but not a Muslim! Then who am I? I am a Palestinian Arab Israeli Christian. My name is Tony Mubarak. Arabic is my mother tongue, and Christianity is my religion. I was created in the image of God; just like every other human, I am no more or less than anyone else.

Above all, I want to thank you for going on this pilgrimage to the hidden bridge. From the Christians of the Holyland—those of us in Israel, Jerusalem, the West Bank and Gaza, as well as our brothers and sisters from Muslim and Jewish backgrounds—it is a tremendous blessing to share the journey with you.

All of us believers (you included!) still carry the aroma of Christ. You need to shake the bottle of perfume before you can smell its odor, and we are being shaken all the time so that the smell of Christ can spread through us down through the centuries.

Jesus spoke with authority and keeps on impressing us every day until He comes back. What does it mean if and when you come to the Holyland, but there is no body of Christ, no Christians to tell you the story of Christ? Don't stay long because He is not here! Go and find Him in your home and church! But He is still here. We, the Holyland Christians, still carry His smell and His message. We are the people you should find. We are the Christians to keep His light shining despite all the challenges.

The Christians in the Holyland are like a jewel that is being polished now and will one day shine brightly, but it needs to be put in the right hands. This is how Christianity has spread and was never defeated throughout the centuries, all because of the power of Christ's love through the middle of all the pain and suffering.

Life isn't meant to be easy; it's meant to be life. It is like a piano with mostly white keys, but there are some black ones that need to be pressed as well. Both of these keys are needed to make a pleasant melody.

As Christian Arabs, we can relate to both, the Muslim world (we speak the same Arabic language thus we can understand them well) and we can relate to the Jewish world as well (for we do believe in the Old Testament, the same book they believe in). We, the Christian Arabs, are the bridge between these two worlds. We often transcend the borders. So, this is another reason why you need to find us.

The Christians of the Holyland are in such a difficult position, caught between Israeli-Jews and Palestinian-Muslims, called to shine the light of Christ to all, despite all the strong political and religious differences. For we know how to promote understanding, our tolerance, and respect among our different communities both Jews and Muslims can contribute to a more peaceful and harmonious world.

In a few years, if we're not careful, the Holyland will be only empty churches of stones for tourists to visit. These places will be like open museums and not churches of local indigenous Christians. This may happen in the next century, if not before.

The Christian tourists are not guests; you are part of the church and coming to the Holyland is a journey to help you discover the roots of your faith. To meet with the local community on Sundays, for example, and to get to chat with the locals makes a huge difference on both sides. We are pivotal as well in connecting the universal church to the mother church in the Holyland to reach all of its people.

I hope this book has challenged you and expanded your thinking. It is essential to pray, true, but then we need to act. Every five minutes, a

EPILOGUE

Christian is persecuted in the Middle East. My hope is that this book will encourage many others to choose to journey to the Holyland and enrich their biblical experience.

This political-religious struggle has been bitter and long for over a century now, and still, we don't have a solution. All attempts from outside have failed. Nevertheless, we need your encouragement and prayers for our politicians to sit down together and talk to both sides.

The solution can come only from within and not be imposed on us from the outside. And we, the Christian Arabs, are vital to make this difference in connecting both sides the Jews and the Muslims, as a third inside party that can understand both.

Thus, I see peace is possible only on the basis of our faith as a common ground. I cannot see any other solution that will bring peace to this place. This is the only common wings that we are under; it must be through our faith. Whether we are Jews, Christians, or Muslims, if we have God's peace in Christ, as our Lord Jesus Himself prayed, asking that all might be one even as He and the Father were one, then we can find peace.

We, as Middle Eastern Christians, form the backbone of the Arab and Levant, for the Arab world will not be able to survive without Christ. Unless we stay close to Him and partner with Him in all we do, we will follow our emotions rather than God's presence. Our troubles are real and painful, but His presence is also real and more powerful than our feelings. Our troubles are temporary, and our emotions will change, but God's presence is eternal.

We will not understand everything that happens in our life, but we can trust the fact that God is all-loving and always present. He is with us whatever we go through. As much as we can, we must keep our story alive. We have a story to tell, the story of Jesus and the story of

Epilogue

God's love to humans. It is first and last a love story of the Creator to His creation that our minds could not grasp.

I am ending this book while at home in Jerusalem. I pray that this Hidden Bridge, we the Christians of the Holyland, will be found by the international church. Remember, the Jews and Muslims of the land don't know a lot about each other, but we can be that bridge for both the locals and the international pilgrims, actually for everybody who comes across this bridge.

When you find this Hidden Bridge, all the Christians of the Holyland that I spoke about in Part Two of the book, you need to act and cross it, and when you do, you will discover more beautiful things than you have ever experienced before. Only the Lord keeps this bridge hanging firmly between the Jewish and the Muslim edges throughout all these centuries.

We, the Christians of this land, this HIDDEN BRIDGE, want to challenge you to come and travel to the land, to take the courage to start walking on this hidden bridge, to experience it for yourself and help strengthen it, so that more people can cross on it in their life journey.

It is important to recognize the existence of Christians in the Holyland and to respect their cultural and religious identity. By doing so, we can help to ensure that we feel valued and included in our communities, which can in turn help to enhance our sense of belonging and our overall well-being.

Finally, thank you for taking the time to read the book. I hope you enjoyed this simple message of a Christian Arab from Jerusalem who loves his people and wants to share this love—the love of Christ—with the whole world.

Always in Him,

Tony Mubarak

Bibliography

Rosenberg, Joel. *Inside the Revolution: How the Followers of Jihad, Jefferson, and Jesus Are Battling to Dominate the Middle East and Transform the World.* Tyndale House Publishers, Inc. USA: 2005

Awad, Alex. *Palestinian Memories: The Story of a Palestinian Mother and her People.* Bethlehem Bible College, Palestine: 2008

Bailey, Kenneth E. *Jesus Through Middle Eastern Eyes: Cultural Studies in the Gospels.* InterVarsity Press, USA: 2008

Dr. Mitri Raheb. *Faith in the Face of Empire: The Bible through Palestinian Eyes.* Published by Orbis Books, USA: 2014

Chapman, Colin. *Whose Promised Land? The Continuing Crisis over Israel and Palestine.* Lion Hudson, England: 2015

Walker, Derek. *A Panorama of Prophecy.* Oxford Bible Church, England: 2015

Additional Information and Resources

Stay Connected with Twins Tours:

Website: Visit **www.twintours.com** for more information.

YouTube: Search for "Twins Tours" on YouTube to access a wide range of teachings. Don't forget to subscribe to the video channel.

https://www.youtube.com/twinstours

Podcasts: Enjoy all the teachings from this book and more on Andre's podcast. Listen here: **https://podcasts.apple.com/us/podcast/israel-walking-the-holy-land/id1437523827**

What's App: Contact Andre at +972545231145.

Email: For any inquiries, send an email to **info@twinstours.com**

ADDITIONAL INFORMATION AND RESOURCES

Subscribe to Online Video Courses: Access online video courses at **www.twinstours.com/academy**

Instagram: Follow Andre on Instagram at **https://instagram.com/twinstours**

Join Facebook Group: Connect with others in the Twins Tours Facebook Group at **https://www.facebook.com/groups/278954974433933**

Facebook: Stay updated with Twins Tours on Facebook at **https://www.facebook.com/TwinsToursTravel/**

Twitter: Follow Andre on Twitter at **https://twitter.com/twinstours**

Three Recommended Books about the Holyland to deepen your understanding beyond this book, I highly recommend the following five books:

"Heading to the Holyland: How to Pray, Plan and Prepare for a Life-Changing Journey

"Study Reader Israel: Twins Tours"

"One Friday in Jerusalem" all above Three books are by Andre Moubarak

Additional Information and Resources

You can find these books on Amazon, or on our website: www.twinstours.com/shop

The Story behind our Website - www.twinstours.com

When the COVID-19 pandemic struck in March 2020, travel groups stopped coming to the country, leaving me with nothing to do. As someone who loves my work and is passionate about it, this sudden halt was disheartening.

In my desire to help during this challenging time, I turned to God and sought guidance through prayer. After three days of earnest prayer, I felt led to create "Twins Tours Academy" and develop video courses that allow virtual visits to sites in Israel over ten days. These courses follow a chronological order, starting from Jesus' birth and concluding with His resurrection. To my knowledge, no other tour guide or travel agency offers this comprehensive ten-day tour in chronological order.

Through these online video teachings, I aim to impart the heart and mind of Jesus while providing insight into the culture, customs, and context of Scripture. Over the course of many years, I poured my heart, hard work, and dedication into developing these deep online video teachings, even without expecting monetary compensation. The Academy represents my 20 years of experience as a guide, incorporating abundant resources and information to help you internalize God's Word. Furthermore, it offers a creative way to explore the land when physical visits are not feasible.

Understanding that a ten-day tour in Israel can be financially burdensome, I made these online courses freely accessible through the website. However, if you have been blessed by the content and wish to support our ministry, I invite you to consider becoming a monthly partner. By making a monthly donation of $25, $50, $100, or $250, you will gain unlimited access to my future media projects and books. If you are unable to contribute financially, I kindly request your help in spreading the word about the website to your friends, family, church members, and on social media. www.twinstours.com/give

Twins Tours Academy - Online Courses

Living in Israel, we have had the privilege of guiding Christian groups through the Holyland on a daily basis. However, not everyone has the opportunity to embark on this journey due to various reasons:

1. **Financial constraints**: Traveling to Israel can be expensive, often requiring years of saving to afford the trip.

2. **Physical challenges**: The long flight, extensive walking, and lack of wheelchair accessibility at many Israeli tourist sites make it strenuous and exhausting for some individuals to participate in organized group tours.

3. **Time constraints**: Taking a trip to Israel typically requires a minimum of 8 days, not including travel time, which may be difficult for those unable to take an extended break from work or family obligations.

ADDITIONAL INFORMATION AND RESOURCES

4. **Concerns about the Middle East**: Ongoing uprisings and regional conflicts in the surrounding countries often create anxiety and hesitation about traveling to the Middle East.

5. **Health considerations**: The recent global pandemic and potential future requirements for proof of vaccination or quarantine pose additional challenges to international travel.

We would like to provide you with an immersive online experience that allows you to virtually explore the Holyland. It is essential to emphasize that numerous groups visiting Israel have unfortunately missed out on receiving high-quality educational content during their tours, despite visiting renowned tourist sites. Rather than having the opportunity to delve deeper into each location, they were hurriedly moved from one place to another to fulfill their itinerary.

Why Another Online Course: "Twin Tours Academy"

In these online courses, you will have the flexibility to learn at your own pace, as they are designed to be easily accessible on your devices. Regardless of your location, you can explore the wonders of the Holyland at your preferred time, in the comfort and convenience of your own surroundings.

Through these courses, you will have the opportunity to virtually visit significant biblical sites and gain profound insights. The teachings offered will present the mind and heart of Jesus through the lens of

Middle Eastern perspectives and the cultural and contextual backdrop of the first-century Aramaic Hebraic world.

Our faith finds its roots in the historical, geographical, and archaeological significance of the Holyland, encompassing modern-day Israel, Jordan, Lebanon, Syria, Iraq, and Egypt. This region, often referred to as the "Levant," serves as a geological bridge connecting Africa, Asia, and Europe. It stands as the epicenter of the world, where God chose to reveal Himself, and the accounts of this divine revelation are recorded within the pages of the Bible. It is a story of salvation that unfolded among real people during a specific time in history within this particular region. While the message of salvation spread throughout the world, some indigenous Christians have remained in the Holyland. I am privileged to be descended from these indigenous Christians and honored to share a part of my personal testimony with you.

Tony and Andre, both born and raised in Jerusalem, have spoken the Semitic languages like Jesus and His disciples. The streets of the Old City of Jerusalem served as their childhood playground, where they knew that Jesus performed miracles and taught parables in their own neighborhood. Their family resided along the Via Dolorosa, the path Jesus walked while carrying His cross to Golgotha.

Some Background about the Maronite Community:

Our family belongs to the Maronite Aramaic-speaking Christian community, and we consider ourselves indigenous to the Holyland. We have an ancient and unbroken lineage of following in the footsteps of Jesus and the teachings of the Bible, starting from the early church until the present day. All of our ancestors were Christians from

Lebanon, tracing our roots back to the early days of the church. Our language is Aramaic, specifically with a Syrian dialect, which closely resembles the Aramaic spoken by Jesus Himself in His Galilean dialect. Additionally, I have also learned to speak Hebrew, which came naturally to me as Hebrew, Aramaic, and Arabic are all Semitic languages closely related to one another. Understanding these languages helps me gain a deeper comprehension of Scripture, as Jesus himself would have spoken Hebrew and Aramaic in His daily life.

The Maronite church was established by believers who lived in the ancient region of Greater Syria, near the church of Antioch where the followers of Jesus were first called "Christians." Located in the present-day regions of Lebanon and Syria, they were the immediate neighbors of the Jewish believers in Israel, and from the very beginning, they adopted the prayer style of the Jerusalem Church. This prayer tradition, known as the "Liturgy of Saint James," has been continuously practiced by the Maronite Church to this day, preserving its Aramaic form without external influences from the West, unlike the Roman Catholic Church.

The Maronite tradition is rooted in the practices of the original Jerusalem church, which was led by Jewish disciples of Jesus shortly after His resurrection. In the Book of Acts, we learn that the disciples and believers who remained in Jerusalem continued to pray in the Temple, observe Jewish prayers, honor the Jewish patriarchs, and experienced the excitement of recognizing Jesus as their Messiah within the Jewish context.

As Aramean Christians, we have carefully preserved the ancient prayers and ways of thinking from the 1st century. Therefore, I am able to authentically teach you the original Hebraic context of Scripture, as I belong to this ancient Semitic linguistic heritage and Middle Eastern way of thinking.

It's important to note that Maronites are not Arabs or Palestinians; we are descendants of the Arameans, a group that originated in modern-day Syria several thousand years before Christ. Aramaic, the language spoken by Jesus, has gradually faded away over the centuries, but our Maronite identity and national heritage are firmly rooted in Aramaic Phoenician culture. Interestingly, I have personally taken a DNA ancestry test which confirmed that I am 100% from the Middle East, specifically from modern-day Lebanon and Syria. This means that my ancestors were originally Phoenicians.

Due to my deep connection to the customs, culture, and context of Scripture, I can easily explain and provide insights into these aspects.

We Maronites are not only heirs to an ancient Christian lineage through our ancestry, but we are also Spirit-filled believers and followers of Jesus Christ. We firmly believe in the power of the unchanging Word of God. My approach to teaching Scripture is grounded in a profound understanding and reverence for the Word of God.

www.twinstours.com

What Is Taught in the Online Courses

Through these online courses, we aim to take you on a transformative journey, enabling you to see the land of the Bible through the lens of Jesus' Middle Eastern perspective. With our 20 years of experience as indigenous believers who speak and comprehend the languages of Jesus, we will guide you through an exploration of the 1st century lifestyle in Israel.

Additional Information and Resources

During the courses, we will delve into the intricate details of how the people of the 1st century lived, including their daily routines, dietary practices, attire, occupations, modes of transportation, worship traditions, and methods of communication. By immersing ourselves in their culture, customs, and the broader context of their mindset, we will gain a comprehensive understanding of life during that time. We refer to these as the three C's: culture, customs, and context.

Our ultimate aspiration is that these courses will offer you a deeper comprehension of Jesus, leading to a more profound connection with Him. As a result, we hope that these teachings will bring clarity to your understanding, provide necessary corrections where needed, and offer confirmation to strengthen your personal journey with Jesus.

Please let us know if there's anything else we can assist you with or any specific topics you would like us to cover in these courses.

First C: Culture

Indeed, culture plays a significant role in shaping people's lives, influencing their perspectives, values, humor, loyalties, fears, and hopes. Understanding the cultural context is crucial for grasping the specific meanings of words and expressions within a language. This is especially true when studying the Hebrew language and Jewish culture of Jesus. During the 1st century, Jesus lived in a time when the Temple and its sacrificial system were still operational, while the entire region was under Roman rule.

Jesus, born into a Jewish family in Bethlehem, was raised in Nazareth and immersed in Jewish traditions. He studied the Torah in the local synagogue, adhering to the practices of a Middle Eastern, Galilean, and Torah-observant Jew. He and His family journeyed to the Temple in Jerusalem for the three pilgrimage feasts. Jesus served as a Rabbi in Galilee, teaching in various synagogues. He returned to Jerusalem during the holy festival of Passover, where He ultimately became the sacrificial Lamb of Judah. It is believed that He will return as the victorious Lion of Judah in the future.

When engaging with Scripture and seeking to deepen our relationship with Jesus, understanding His Jewish identity and cultural background becomes invaluable. It provides us with a perspective that differs from our own Western and modern culture. These online courses aim to offer practical insights and information on comprehending Jesus within the context of His 1st century culture. Furthermore, it is worth mentioning that I also have a comprehensive online course available that explores the differences between Eastern and Western cultures.

Second C: Customs

Customs are fundamental aspects of a culture, comprising patterns of behavior that are followed and upheld by its members. Often, individuals adhere to customs without fully comprehending their origins or underlying reasons. Customs serve a crucial role in fostering a sense of affiliation and belonging within communities, groups, and organizations, contributing to social cohesion. As customs are deeply ingrained in societal dynamics, they gradually evolve into the accepted norms of a given society.

By embracing and practicing customs, individuals participate in shared traditions, rituals, and behaviors that strengthen the bonds among community members. These customs help to establish a collective identity, preserve cultural heritage, and maintain social order. They provide individuals with a sense of continuity, connecting them to the past, and shaping the present and future of their culture.

Understanding customs within a specific cultural context allows for a deeper appreciation of the values, beliefs, and social dynamics of a society. It enables individuals to engage with others more effectively, respect diversity, and foster social harmony.

Third C: Context

Understanding the context of words and passages is indeed crucial when interpreting Scripture. Each verse in the Bible carries a specific historical context, encompassing cultural elements, customs, the time period, the author, the intended audience, geographical and political circumstances, as well as the occasion and purpose of the writing. Examining the historical context allows for a clearer understanding of the circumstances surrounding events and teachings that may be unfamiliar to us in our current time.

In your signature course, "The Lord's Prayer in Aramaic," participants will have the opportunity to learn how to read and write Aramaic. This will enable them to recite the Lord's Prayer in Jesus' own language, experiencing the depth and beauty of the original Aramaic sentences spoken by Jesus himself, just as he did 2000 years ago.

Additionally, there is another course available for learning biblical Hebrew, consisting of seven lessons. Biblical Hebrew is the primary language used in the 39 books of the Tanach (Hebrew Bible), also known as the Old Testament. Hebrew is written and read from right to left, with its unique alphabet. Hebrew letters do not have uppercase and lowercase forms. The Babylonian script, commonly used in modern Hebrew Bibles, is employed in this course. Vowel points are utilized to indicate vowel sounds, and it should be noted that Hebrew letters and vowels can be pronounced in different ways due to various dialects. The course teaches the Modern dialect, which is considered the standard way of speaking Hebrew in present-day Israel.

The objective of these language courses is to provide beginners with a solid foundation in understanding and utilizing Aramaic and Hebrew. They aim to equip participants with essential knowledge that can serve as a basis for more advanced language studies in the future.

Moreover, there will be additional courses available, including the historical geography of the land of the Bible, exploring the differences between Eastern and Western cultures, and delving into the significance of the Shema, the most important Jewish prayer in the Old Testament. These courses will offer opportunities to learn phrases in Aramaic and Hebrew that scholars agree were likely spoken by Jesus himself.

www.twinstours.com/academy

Acquired Learning

By engaging in these courses, you will gain valuable insights into how God has worked throughout history, archaeology, and the geography of the land of the Bible. The transformative power of these teachings lies in their ability to help you think more like Middle Eastern Jesus. As you delve into the culture, customs, and context of Jesus' time, you will develop a deeper understanding of His identity. This understanding, in turn, will enable you to grasp the significance of your own life in relation to Him.

The courses aim to bring about a transformation in your thinking and perspective, aligning it with the teachings and mindset of Jesus. This process of renewal aligns with the scriptural exhortation to be transformed by the renewing of your mind (Romans 12:2). By immersing yourself in these teachings, you will experience a profound impact, particularly if you have a hunger to deepen your spiritual walk and gain a greater understanding of the stories within the Bible.

Embarking on this journey through the online courses will yield three significant results: clarity, correction, and confirmation. The teachings will bring clarity to your understanding, allowing you to grasp the deeper meaning and significance of biblical narratives. They will also provide correction, aligning your perspectives with the truth and authenticity of Jesus' teachings and life. Finally, these courses will offer confirmation, strengthening your faith and affirming the truths you already hold.

Clarity

These online courses provide clarity in your Christian walk by helping you understand Scripture in a clearer way, eliminating confusion and bringing focus to your life.

Correction

Through these online courses, your understanding of the Word of God will be corrected. Sadly, our current culture often rejects correction, emphasizing self-centeredness and resistance to guidance. Even within the Christian community, the desire for personal autonomy can hinder the acceptance of correction. Yet, a gentle rebuke has the power to positively impact the soul.

This truth applies to all believers, as we navigate relationships that sometimes call for biblical correction. While it may be challenging, it is an integral part of expressing love in accordance with Scripture (2 Timothy 3:16-17).

Confirmation

Enrolling in these courses will bring confirmation to your faith. The Holy Spirit empowers us to live out our faith in every aspect of life and to bear witness to Christ in all circumstances.

In our present culture, characterized by anxiety, disagreements, doubts, and the denial of Christian beliefs, the challenge lies in whether we will obey Christ or conform to the prevailing culture. These online courses will anchor you and instill greater confidence in your Christian journey.

Confirmation of the Word of God serves to establish a stronger connection with the Holy Spirit and fosters a deeper sense of unity within the church community, our fellow brothers and sisters in Christ (Hebrews 4:12).

It is crucial to embrace both the Word and the Spirit. We cannot prioritize the Holy Spirit while disregarding the Word of God. Both aspects are essential as the Word itself is the expression of the Spirit. Scripture, the Word of God, affirms our faith, nurturing its growth, depth, and maturity within the core of our being.

How the Courses Work

By enrolling in these video courses, I will serve as your personal tour guide and instructor. These courses are structured into multiple lessons and offer a comprehensive learning experience. Packed with insightful teachings, maps, presentations, and captivating pictures of the Holyland, they will enhance your understanding of the Bible.

To ensure a continuous learning journey, a new video teaching will be delivered to your email inbox every month. This regular distribution of content will enable you to steadily deepen your knowledge and engagement with the material.

www.twinstours.com/academy

Who Benefits from the Courses

These online courses are specifically designed for church leaders, ministry leaders, elders, pastors, and individuals seeking to deepen their spiritual walk through a comprehensive understanding of Scripture. Drawing from my extensive experience guiding believers on tours of the Holyland, I have dedicated countless hours to curating

Additional Information and Resources

and developing these courses to be accessible and easily comprehensible.

The "Twins Tours Academy" courses offer a transformative spiritual journey through the land of the Bible, with a focus on personal growth and a deeper relationship with God. You can join me in these enlightening Zoom classes, and I invite you to RSVP for the next free lesson at **www.twinstours.com/webinars**

ADDITIONAL INFORMATION AND RESOURCES

More Books Written By Andre Moubarak my Twin Brother:

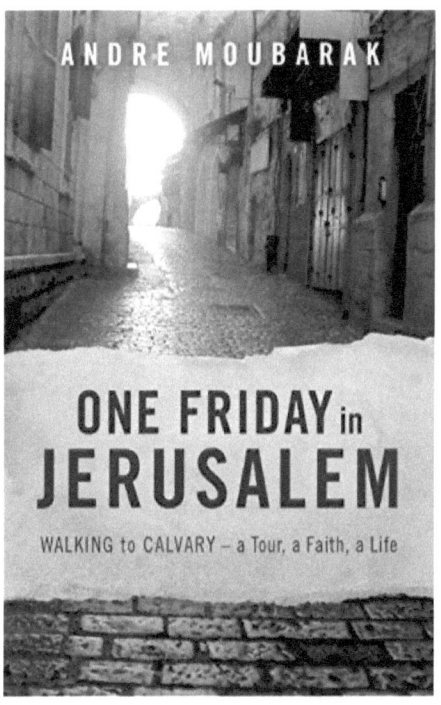

Step into the sandals of Jesus and experience the profound journey of *One Friday in Jerusalem*. This captivating tour book immerses you in the sights, sounds, and emotions as Jesus carries His cross along the arduous half-mile path to Calvary. Feel the sweat on your brow, inhale the scents of the bustling crowd, hear the commanding voices of soldiers, and confront the agonizing reality of the crucifixion. Andre, a member of a marginalized community in a land divided by ethnicity, shares why each station of the cross holds deep significance.

One Friday in Jerusalem goes beyond a mere tour guide, offering unique Middle Eastern perspectives on the Bible. Packed with historical, cultural, geographical, archaeological, and spiritual insights, it takes you on a profound reflection of Jesus' passion. Through the remarkable and true stories of Andre, who intimately understands the sorrows and struggles of the Via Dolorosa, you will also encounter the transformative power of the risen Christ—a source of joy, hope, and life-changing impact.

Second book written by Andre Moubarak

Touring the Holyland is a must-have guide for Tour Leaders, Pastors, and anyone planning to bring a group to Israel. This concise book covers everything from legal and ethical considerations to cultural insights, providing you with the necessary tools to become a skilled and equipped Tour Leader. Whether managing a group in Israel or the West Bank, Touring the Holyland will help you navigate the process and ensure a successful and impactful experience for your group.

Visit our website, **www.twinstours.com/shop**, or find the book on platforms like Amazon.

www.ingramcontent.com/pod-product-compliance
Lightning Source LLC
Chambersburg PA
CBHW030226100526
44585CB00012BA/259